Trance Scripts

———————◆———————

Trance Scripts

Scripts for the Professional Hypnotherapist

Randy J. Hartman, M.A.

Writers Club Press
San Jose New York Lincoln Shanghai

Trance Scripts
Scripts for the Professional Hypnotherapist

All Rights Reserved © 2000 by Randy J. Hartman

No part of this book may be reproduced or transmitted in any form or by any means, graphic, electronic, or mechanical, including photocopying, recording, taping, or by any information storage retrieval system, without the permission in writing from the publisher.

Writers Club Press
an imprint of iUniverse.com, Inc.

For information address:
iUniverse.com, Inc.
620 North 48th Street, Suite 201
Lincoln, NE 68504-3467
www.iuniverse.com

ISBN: 0-595-14070-X

Printed in the United States of America

Cross reference of script application

Script Name	Application	Page
Deep Muscle Relaxation	Learning relaxation	1
Muscle Relaxation	Learning to focus inward	6
Guided Imagery	Basic trance induction	8
Escalator Technique	Basic trance induction	11
Confusion Induction	Basic trance induction	15
Piggyback Induction	Basic trance induction	17
Anxiety Script Panic Attacks	General Anxiety	18
The Strawberry	Reduce Compulsive/Stress	20
Blue Sleep	Insomnia	22
Journey of Learning	Improve Positive Decisions	23
View of Life	Insight Building	26
Low Self-Esteem	Building Self-Esteem	28
Wonderland	Building Self-Esteem	30
Self-Esteem Script	Building Self-Esteem	32
Adjusting Your Thermostat	Self-Acceptance	34
Your Museum	Self-Acceptance	36
Fail Safe	Fear of Failure/Tests	38
Craving Again	For Clients in Recovery	40
Balloon Technique	Letting go of Desires	43
Smoking Abstinence Script	Stop Smoking	45
Blended Stop Smoking Script	Stop Smoking	49

Dogs	Procrastination	52
Bandits	Procrastination	54
Chronic Pain Management	Pain Management	55
Long Term Pain Management	Pain Management	57
Brief Pain Management	Pain Management	60
Ulcer and Colitis Script	Ulcer & Colitis	63
Healing Migraine Headache Script	Headache Relief	65
Tree Ants	Increase Immune System	66
Rafting	Controlling Hypertension	68
Multiple Personalities	MPD's	70
Merging Script	M.P.D's	72
Dreams	Survivors of Sexual Assault	74
Meeting the Inner Child	Experiencing Inner Child	76
Abusive Childhood Issues	Resolving Abuse	78
Saying Good-Bye	Resolving Abuse	79
Letting Go	Resolving Abuse	81
The Rose	Relationships	82
The Dance	Risk Taking	84
Emotional Droughts	Relationships	87
Playground in the Mind	Relationship Trust	89
Jealous Ways	Resolving Jealousy	91
Territory	Resolving Jealousy	93
Treasures of the Past	Grieving	95
Turtle	Relationship Trust	97
The Flat Tire	Accepting Others	99

Introduction

◆

The intent and purpose of this book is to provide the Hypnotherapy Practitioner with a ready resource of scripts that can serve their clients in a quick and meaningful way.

These scripts are not being offered as a cure for any problems that clients bring to you. These scripts are merely stepping stones to help you move the client through the helping process in a "user-friendly" and rapid manner. It is important to remember that follow-up after hypnotic intervention is essential to helping the client achieve a successful outcome.

The real value in these scripts is that your client does not have to take immediate ownership for the problem talked about in the script. They can see similarities in the story with their own life that they can learn from and draw upon in the future. Sometimes these metaphors are described as seeing a segment of one's life in a movie where they don't have to be one of the actors.

The secondary value in using scripts is that it enhances the hypnotherapist's ability and self-confidence. Especially with therapists that are relatively new to the field, scripts have proven to be very useful in gaining the self-confidence needed to move forward in this field. These scripts/metaphors can be used in or out of hypnotic trance, although I recommend using them in a medium state of trance. By having your client in trance you can eliminate the daily chatter in the mind and have the client focus more effectively on the story.

It is important to allow the clients to draw their own interpretation of the metaphor. It is all too easy for the new therapist to try and shape the client's interpretation of the metaphor, but we must allow the client to arrive at their own meaning. It is good to process the experience with them after trance, but never allow yourself to offer your interpretation of the metaphor. Every client's "Model of the World" differs, so it is essential to process with the client after trance, perhaps considering other, more meaningful metaphors in the future.

With any of these scripts in this book, please feel free to alter them to fit your own particular linguistic style of hypnotic patter. Keeping in mind that some words may need to be substituted depending on the level of your client's intellectual functioning. It is very helpful if you take time prior to trance work to read the script out loud to yourself to arrive at your own linguistic comfort level with the information.

Constructing Your Own Metaphors

In this section we will explore the dynamics of understanding, creating and tailoring metaphors for your clients. The uses of metaphors are unlimited in nature; the uses generally assist the client with an entirely different non-threatening look at their situation. In the metaphor the client can look at a similar situation to theirs, and hear ways they might reach a positive outcome with their situation.

The working definition of a metaphor is an object, activity, or idea treated as a metaphor or a figure of speech in which a word or phrase literally denoting one kind of object or idea is used in place of another to suggest a likeness (or analogy) between them. Examples of the sources of such stories include epic poems, novels, poetry, fairytales, fables, songs, movies, jokes and gossip. The metaphor provides the client the opportunity to get out of the trees and take a look at the forest they have been wandering around in.

The one basic fundamental characteristic of a therapeutic metaphor is that the characters and events which occur in the story are equivalent with those individuals and events which characterize the client's situation. The term for this is "Isomorphism", or to create a situation that is "isomorphic" to the client's situation.

To formulate a basic metaphor there are three basic steps that need to occur;

1. Gather Information:
   a. Identify the significant persons involved.
   b. Identify their interpersonal relationship.
   c. Identify the events that are characteristic of the problem situation.
   d. Have the client specify what changes are desired.
   e. Ensure that the changes are well formed and positive.
   f. Identify what the client has done in the past to cope with the problem, or what stops the client from making the desired changes.

2. Build the Metaphor:
   a. Select a context.
   b. Populate and plot the metaphor so that it is isomorphic in nature.
   c. Determine a resolution to end the metaphor with.

3 Tell It:
   a. Using the syntactic patterns of:
   b. Lack of referential index.
   c. Unspecified verbs.
   d. Nominalizations.
   e. Imbedded commands and verbal marking.

The people involved in the actual situation can become other people, trying to pair the male with male roles and the female with the female roles if gender is mentioned in the metaphor. The people could also become objects instead of people. Allow yourself total freedom in constructing a metaphor. The problem in the metaphor should be of equal importance of the real problem situation. Don't be shy about adding great detail in telling the story, such as visual, auditory, feelings, and even odors. At the end of the metaphor offer a model solution for the client to consider. Offering more than one solution often will create only confusion for your client, and then no action or outcome will be initiated.

When employing a metaphor in trance, initiate the trance and take the client to a medium state. Read the client the metaphor slowly, continuing to pace their breathing. This will allow the client to automatically move into a state of somnambulism during the story. By also reading the script slowly you will allow the client to process the information in their "Model of the World" as they receive it. You should remain ever mindful of your client's linguistic abilities, or lack of them. It would be to easy to construct a metaphor with words that the client may not comprehend. This serves to reinforce the idea that we as therapists need to meet our clients at their "Model of the World".

Dr Milton Erickson was a true pioneer in the use of metaphors. One day while Dr Erickson was lecturing a group of new students, a student asked him the following question, "What is the essence of being hypnotherapist?" Dr Erickson replied with the following story: When he was a young man, standing on the side of the street, he spied a horse that came wondering into town. Young Milton didn't recognize the horse or have a clue as to who the owner was, so Milton mounted the horse and turned him back down the road the horse had traveled. Every time the horse strayed from the road, Milton would pull on the horse's neck to bring it back to the middle of the road. After traveling for several miles the horse stopped at a farmhouse, the horse's owner came out and thanked Milton for bring his horse back to where it belonged. The owner asked Milton, "How did you know where to bring the horse?" Milton replied, "I didn't know but the horse knew where he belonged, I just kept him on the road until he got here".

User Friendly Instructions

This book was written with the thought that only those practitioners trained in Hypnotherapy would utilize it as a resource for helping their clients.

When a person writes a book it is almost like having a baby, and of course, you wouldn't want anyone to handle your baby without some instruction or guidance. Therefore, I am writing these "User Friendly" instructions for the use of this book. This book was put together with the K.I.S.S. principle in mind: Keep It Short and Simple. As a testament to that idea, I have bookcases full of books that are wonderful, but don't really make a lot of sense.

All of these scripts and metaphors are simple and fairly easy to apply to your clients. Please bear in mind the following points when utilizing this material;

1. The scripts are double-spaced for easy reading and provide you room to make script changes to facilitate your client and your style.
2. All of these scripts are not wrote in stone, you are definitely encouraged to be flexible and make changes as you see fit and feel the need.
3. Most every script has a note that says you need to continue to pace your client's breathing pattern during the reading of the script. Please do not take that literally, as it is nearly impossible to read a script and watch the client's breathing pattern. Instead, read the

script slowly, very slowly. After using a script a few times you will find you probably won't even need to use the book except for occasional reference.
4. Do not always expect a positive change in your client after using these scripts once. I recommend that you consider using the same script at least three times for maximum results over three sessions.
5. \Never consider any script or metaphor as the only treatment approach you will need for your client. These are adjunctive tools of therapy only. In some wonderful instances you will find that the scripts and metaphors fit the bill, but it is safer to assume that other interventions will be needed.
6. For maximum effective impact with your client, it is recommended you design specific scripts and metaphors for the client and their situation.

Deep Muscle Relaxation Technique

◆

The numbers of seconds to pause is denoted by the number in parentisis (8).

Welcome to this session. During the next 30 minutes we will work our way through deep muscle relaxation training. The end result of this session is for you to have a heightened sense of awareness of what your body feels like to be fully relaxed. This technique alone will not teach you everything you need to know. It is imperative that you practice all three phases of this program.

We will begin by having you assume a comfortable position. You can either be sitting down in a chair or lying down. If you use a chair, try to make it one with arms, if lying down, do not use a pillow. If your clothing is too tight and uncomfortable, loosen it slightly now (4). Settle back now as comfortable as you can (4). Focus your attention on my voice (3). As other thoughts drift into your mind, let them drift away and continue to focus on my voice only (4). (Spend four minutes talking the client through a deep breathing exercise). As you relax, clench your right fist, now clench your fist tighter and tighter, and study the tension in your right fist and forearm. You can feel the tension become uncomfortable in your right fist and forearm. You can feel the tension become uncomfortable in your right fist as you fist as you keep it tightly clenched (3). Now relax (4). Let the fingers of your right hand become loose (5). Observe the contrast in the feelings of your right hand (5). Let yourself go and try to become more relaxed all over (5). Once more again, clench your right fist really tight (3). Hold it tight (3). Now notice the tension again, it feels very tight and uncomfortable (2). Now let go (2). Relax, straighten out your fingers (3). Notice the difference once more (10). Now we will repeat that with your left hand and forearm (2). Clench your left fist while the rest of your body relaxes (3). Clench your fist tight and feel the tension (3). Now relax (5). Again, enjoy the contrast in feelings (4). Let your mind focus on that feeling of relaxation. Repeat that once more, clench your left fist (3). Make your fist very tight and tense (3). Now relax and feel the difference (4). Slowly straighten out your fingers (10). Clench both fists now (3). Tight, and tighter (2). Both fists tense, forearms tense, study the sensation (2). Relax now (2). Let the feelings of relaxation flow into both hands (2). Straighten out your fingers and feel the relaxation (3). Continue relaxing your hands and forearms more and more (3). Now bend both your elbows and tense your biceps by pulling your hands towards your shoulders (3). Tense them tighter and study the feelings of tension (5). Now straighten out your arms (4). Let them relax, and now feel the difference again (3). Let the relaxation develop (8). Once more, tense your biceps (4). Hold that tension and observe it carefully (4). Straighten your arms and allow the feelings of relaxation to flow into yours arms (4). Relax to the best of your ability (8). Now straighten your arms so that you feel the most tension in the tricep muscle along the back of your arms (3). Now relax (5). Move your arms back into a comfortable position (5). Let the relaxation flow on its own accord (8). Your arms should feel comfortably heavy as you allow the relaxation to flow (5). Once more, straighten your arms so that you feel the tension in your triceps (8). Let your arms relax again and focus on the comfortable heavy feeling of relaxation in your arms (6). Now let's focus on pure relaxation in the arms without any tension. Move your arms into a comfortable position and let them relax (8). Let the relaxation flow into your arms (3). Focus on that nice warm feeling in your arms (10). Even when your arms seem fully relaxed, try to let your arms achieve a deeper level of relaxation (12). Now we will move upwards to the head and shoulders (2). We will start by letting all your muscles go loose and heavy. Just settle back quietly and comfortably. Wrinkle up your forehead now (3). Wrinkle it tighter (5). Now stop wrinkling your forehead (4). Relax and allow it to smooth out (3). Picture your entire forehead and scalp becoming smoother as the relaxation increases (10). Now frown and crease your brows and study the tension (6). Let go of the tension once again, smooth out your forehead once more (10). Now close your eyes tighter and tighter (5). Feel the tension (3). Now relax your eyes (4). keep your eyes closed gently, comfortably and notice the relaxation (10). Now clench your jaws (10). Relax your jaws now, let your lips part slightly (6). Appreciate the feeling of relaxation (12). Now press your tongue hard against the roof of your mouth (4). Look for the tension (4). All right, let your tongue return to a comfortable and relaxed position (10). Now press your lips together (4). Tighter and tighter (4). Relax your lips; note the contrast between tension and relaxation (8). Feel the relaxation all over your face (8). Now to attend to your neck muscles, press your head back as far as it can go and feel the tension in your neck (3). Roll it to the right and feel the tension shift (3). Now roll it to the left (3). Straighten your head and bring it forward (3). Press your chin against your chest (4). Let your head return to a comfortable position, and study the relaxation (5). Let the relaxation develop (10). Now shrug your shoulders straight up (4). Hold the tension (4). Drop your shoulders slowly and feel the relaxation (4). Feel your neck and shoulders relaxing (8). Shrug your shoulders up and forward (4). Now back, Feel the tension in your shoulders and in your upper back (4). Drop your shoulders slowly once more and relax (6). Let the relaxation spread deeply into your shoulders, right into your back muscles (6). Relax your neck and throat, and your jaw and other facial areas as the pure relaxation takes over and goes deeper (3). Deeper, even again, let your stomach out. Continue to breathe normally and easily and feel the gentle massaging action all over your chest and stomach (12). Now pull your stomach in again and hold the tension (8).

Release the tension (8). once more pull in your stomach fully and feel the tension (8). Now relax your stomach fully (3). Let the tension dissolve as the relaxation grows deeper (6). Each time you breathe out notice the rhythmic relaxation both in your lungs and in your stomach (10). Notice how your chest and stomach relaxes more and more (8). Try and let go of all the muscle tension anywhere in your body (12). Now direct your attention to your lower back (3). Arch up your back, make your lower back quite hollow, and feel the tension along your spine (4). Now settle back comfortably again, relaxing the lower back (10). Arch your back up again and feel the tension as you do so. Try to keep the rest of your body relaxed as possible. Try to localize the tension throughout your lower back area (2). Relax once more (3). Relax your upper back (6). Spread the relaxation to your stomach (6). Now to your chest (6). Now to your shoulders (6). Now to your arms (6). Now to your facial area (6). These parts are relaxing further and further, and further and even deeper (6). Let it flow as a warm, heavy, comfortable feeling (12). Let go of all tensions and just relax (8). Now flex your buttocks and thighs. Flex your thighs by pressing down your heels as hard as you can (6). Relax and note the difference (8). Straighten your knees and flex your thigh muscles again, hold the tension (6). Relax your hips and thighs (8). Allow the relaxation to proceed on its own (10). Press your feet and toes downwards, away from your face, so that calf muscles become tense, study that tension (6). Relax your feet and calves (8). This time, bend your feet away from your face so that you feel tension along your shins (6) bring your toes back up (2) relax again. (6) Keep relaxing for a while (6), now let yourself relax further all over (6). Relax your feet (6). Relax, your ankles now (6). Relax your calves now (6). Relax your shins now (6). Relax your knees now (6). Relax your thighs now (6). Relax your buttocks now (6). Relax your hips now (6). Feel the heaviness of your lower body as you relax still further (8). Let go now, more and more (4). Feel that relaxation all over. Let it proceed to your upper back (6). Keep relaxing more and more deeply (12). Make sure that no tension has crept into your throat (2). Relax your neck and your jaws and all your facial muscles (4). Keep relaxing your whole body like that for a while. Let yourself totally relax (12). Now you can become twice as relaxed by taking in a really deep breath and slowly exhaling (6). Close your eyes so that you become less aware of objects and movements around you, and prevent any surface tensions from developing (8). Breathe in deeply and feel yourself becoming heavier (6). Take a long deep breath and let it out very slowly (6). Feel how heavy and relaxed you have become (12). The relaxation is flowing through you in a warm and comfortable way (30). In a state of perfect relaxation you should feel unwilling to move a single muscle in your body (3). Think about the effort that would be required to raise your right arm, as you think about raising your right arm, see if you can notice any tensions that might have crept into your right shoulder and your arm (6). Now you decide not to lift your arm, but to continue relaxing (12). Observe the relief and the disappearance of the tension (6). Just continue relaxing like that (12). When you wish to get up, count backward from five to one (6). You should then feel fine and refreshed, wide-awake and calm, slowly open your eyes and look about (4). Flex your fingers and toes slightly. Now in a slow and easy manner, you can bring yourself to your feet (6).

It may be necessary for you to repeat this exercise several times to develop a strong sense of awareness of what your body feels like to be relaxed. The value of this exercise is for you to develop a heightened sense of awareness of the feelings of relaxation and the feelings of tension.

Muscle Relaxation Technique

◆

Welcome to the second in a series of your relaxation training. Before moving into the second phase of this program lets take a minute to review the first phase. Hopefully by now you have repeated the first phase of relaxation and tension. During this phase I want you to mentally recall the feelings you experienced during the first session.

Recall it slowly (10). Tighten and loosen your muscles if needed to re-awaken the feeling of relaxation (10). Settle back, and make yourself comfortable (15). Also recall the breathing exercises now that we are prepared (15). Lets move on (5). Begin with your feet, focus on your toes and feet, focus on that comfortable, warm, heavy feeling (10). If you find distracting thoughts drift into your mind, let them drift on by, don't try to force the thoughts out of your mind (3). Just let them drift on by (10). Focus now on the calves of your legs (10). Feel them grow heavier and heavier (10). Feel the tension drift away and that heavy comfortable feeling flow in (15). Now let that nice feeling of relaxation flow slowly upwards (15). You can feel it slowly working into your thighs (10). You're now feeling that nice warm heavy feeling spread throughout your thighs (10). Feel your thigh grow heavier and heavier (10). Feel the tension drift away and that heavy comfortable feeling flow freely (15). If you find distracting thoughts coming into your has drifted out of your arms and hands now, and the warm heavy feeling is flowing freely (10). Your arms and hands continue to grow warm and heavy (10). Let the feeling of relaxation go deeper and deeper (20). Now let your mind slowly move to focus on your neck and scalp (15). Let the warm comfortable feeling spread up through your neck and into your scalp (10). The tension is slowly drifting away (12). Now the warm comfortable feeling is flowing and feeling better and better (12). Slowly you feel the warmth move you deeper and deeper into relaxation (15). The feeling of relaxation is now drifting down into your facial muscles (10). The tension is drifting out now and that warm relaxed feeling is increasing (15). Now the warm heavy comfortable feeling is flowing with warmth and comfort (30). Now you are feeling that warm, heavy, comfortable feeling engulf your entire body (45). The feeling flows so freely into the warm wonderful feeling of relaxation (60). Now, very slowly count backwards from five to one (10). Now slowly move your toes (5). Now also move your fingers slightly (5). Open your eyes and slowly look about you (4). At this time you will start to feel more alert and refreshed (6).

You may feel free to get up now and move about. It is recommended that you practice this technique several times before moving on to the guided imagery phase.

Guided Imagery

◆

During this session we will focus on guided imagery as a means of relaxation. This is the third and final teaching phase in progressive relaxation techniques. We start this session with a reflective look back to the sessions of deep muscle techniques and muscle relaxation. Try to recall in your mind the feelings you experienced during these exercises. The bold (0) denote pauses in seconds.

    Assume a comfortable position before you begin to form the mental image of your body relaxing (6). Loosen any tight clothing and let the warm comfortable feeling of relaxation take over (12). If any distracting thoughts enter your mind, let them drift on bye and continue to focus on the sound of my voice, and that warm, heavy and comfortable feeling that is starting to move through your body (15). If you have trouble recalling that feeling of relaxation at this time, stop briefly and perform phase one again of the deep muscle relaxation technique until you have developed a re-awareness of relaxation in your body (15). Now mentally recreate that feeling of relaxation in your body (10). Let it begin with your toes (10). Slowly, that warm comfortable feeling starts moving upwards (10). Now moving into the calves of your legs to your mind. They can also just drift on by, the only thing that is important, is hearing the sound of my voice. The sound of my voice can go with you. The sound of my voice can give you the comfort and relaxation that you so richly deserve, as you continue to relax. Letting go a little more, going a little deeper, deeper yet, into that beautiful state of relaxation enjoying all of these wonderful feelings as they just increase. Slowly, very wonderfully, you can notice that your breathing has slowed down to a very slow comfortable pace. Feeling so comfortable so calm, so serene, such a wonderful state of serenity feeling yourself letting go, relaxing more. Going deeper, deeper into that wonderful feeling, such

a beautiful feeling the sense of calmness, complete relaxation. Slowly gently going perhaps another level deeper gently descending into a more beautiful state of relaxation moving at a pace that is comfortable for you, deeper allowing yourself to let go, more, gradually, peacefully moving deeper. You may notice that some of the sounds around you may fade out, or fade in, and that's really all right as you continue to hear the sound of my voice as you continue to let go. relaxing deeper moving yet another level deeper. As you

continue to relax more, you can enjoy even more the wonderful feelings of trance, allowing yourself to drift another level deeper. How very beautiful, very calm very peaceful, how wonderful, as you just continue to let go, relaxing more, slowly moving yet another level deeper. In your mind I would like you to find a special place. A place where you can be comfortable, safe, very secure this is your special place, you can add to or take away from your special place you can allow only the people you want there, because this is your special place. Notice for a moment all the sights and sounds, perhaps even nice odors, enjoy the colors, enjoy the things you have surrounded yourself with knowing that in your special place you are safe, secure and very comfortable as you keep that special place in your mind. You can allow yourself to go even deeper as you see yourself in that special place, you can also see a pretty (color) balloon. This pretty balloon is filled with helium tied to a string that is attached to your finger. What a pretty balloon. You can see it there, tied to your finger and tugging at your finger as it playfully tugs at you finger, it will slowly lift it in a playful and wonderful way, such a pretty balloon. Watching it playfully tugging and pulling your finger upwards, how very nice, knowing that you can gradually now, slip one level deeper, so wonderfully deep, enjoying how very wonderful you feel, enjoying your special place, and the pretty balloon. The balloon is still playfully tugging and pulling your finger upwards, still enjoying all those wonderful feelings of being in trance, feeling so calm, serene, so peaceful, now as you let yourself go. You can still move one level deeper, deeper into those beautiful feelings.

(Terminate or proceed as needed)

(Consider reinforcing the post-hypnotic suggestion three times at three different depths Also reinforce the suggestion after you have brought them half way up out of trance)

(When bringing them up from trance, pace your numbers according to their inhale, elicit words from the client to prevent them from slipping back into trance even deeper)

Escalator Technique

◆

This hypnotic script has many deepening features built into it. Simply have the client relax and close their eyes and begin reading the script while you pace their breathing pattern throughout the trance experience.

Take a comfortable position in your chair. Close your eyes and breathe deeply three times. Now that you are comfortable, you will listen closely to my voice and follow all the suggestions given. Your eyes are now closed, take another deep breath, hold it a few seconds, and let it out. Mentally say to yourself, relax deeply, relax deeply, relax deeply. The more you can relax, and the more you concentrate, the deeper you will go into hypnosis. Let all your muscles go as loose and limp as possible. To do this, start with your right leg, tighten the muscles first, make the leg rigid, then let it relax from your toe right up to your hip. Then tighten the muscles of the left leg, let that leg relax from the toes up to the hip. Let the stomach and abdominal area relax, then your chest and breathing muscles. The muscles of your back can loosen…your shoulders and neck muscles relaxing. often we have tension in these areas. Let all these muscles relax. Now your arms right down to your finger tips. Even your facial muscles will relax, relaxation is so pleasant and comfortable. Let go completely and enjoy the relaxation. All tension seems to drain away and you soon find a listlessness creeping over you, with a sense of comfort and well being. As you relax more and more, you will slip deeper and deeper into hypnosis. Your arms and legs may develop a feeling of heaviness, or instead you find your whole body feeling very light, as though you are floating on a soft cloud. Allow yourself to experience any such sensation you are having for a minute. Just let yourself go and feel the sensation of floating, or heaviness, or any other sensation you are experiencing (ten second pause). Now listen to me and imagine that you are standing at the top of an escalator such as those found in stores. See the steps moving down in front of you, and you see the railings. I am going to count from ten to zero, as I start to count, imagine that you are stepping on the escalator, standing there with your hands on the railing while the steps move down in front of you, taking you with them, if you prefer, you can imagine a staircase or an elevator instead. If you have any difficulty visualizing the escalator or staircase or elevator just the count itself will take you deeper and deeper (Slowly). Ten, now you step on and start going down, nine…eight…seven…six, going deeper and deeper with each count. Five…four…three, still deeper. Two…one…and zero. Now you step off at the bottom and you will continue to go deeper still with each breath you take, deeper and deeper with each breath. You are so relaxed and so comfortable. Let go still more, notice your breathing, probably it is now slower and you are breathing more from the bottom of your lungs and abdominal breathing, As you go deeper into hypnosis, my voice may seem to drift away from you as though it were coming from a great distance, but you shall continue to hear it and pay attention to the suggestions I shall make to you. You will be able to respond to these suggestions even though you are very relaxed and very comfortable (Slowly). Now you can imagine yourself to be strolling down the hall to a special room. A special room in your own mind as you see yourself strolling down the hall, feeling fine, feeling pleasant and relaxed, you can indicate to yourself when you reach the room, you can have it any way you wish it to be. It can be large or small, light or dark, cool or warm, furnished in any way you wish so that it is pleasant, comfortable and attractive. Now, approaching the door to this special room, now seeing yourself opening the door, entering the room, and closing the door. You can arrange yourself in any position that is comfortable, sitting, lying down, or strolling about. As you see yourself in this situation, you can allow yourself to go deeper and deeper, into a very deep state of concentration, a very deep state of relaxation. You know that you can always return to this special room in your mind when you wish to do so. You will be able to learn to use these techniques and these procedures for your own benefit and your own welfare. Now let yourself experience going deeper and deeper into trance. Just pay attention to your breathing, notice how deep and regular your breathing is, you can go deeper into hypnosis with each breath you take, let each breath carry you deeper and deeper and deeper. Just like going to sleep except that you will keep hearing my voice and following my instructions. Now, continue to go deeper into hypnosis, to become more and more comfortable with each breath that you take. Breathing rhythmically and deeply, going deeper with each breath, let yourself go completely now, deeper and deeper, now that you are deeply relaxed, I want you to remain that way for a few minutes while you have an interesting and pleasant experience. I will not tell you what to experience, you can have the kind of experience that you choose to have, it may be a surprise to you, it may be a feeling or a memory, or a thought you just let yourself experience it and enjoy it. As you have this experience you can go deeper and deeper into hypnosis. Now take a few minutes to let yourself experience whatever happens (two minute pause). In a few moments you will be able to complete the thought, feeling or memory. Now imagine that you are standing at the top of an escalator. See the steps moving down in front of you, and see the railings. I am going to count from ten to zero, as I start to count, imagine that you are stepping on to the escalator, standing there with your hands on the railings while the steps move down in front of you, taking you with them. Ten…now you step on and start going down, nine…eight…seven…six…going deeper and deeper with each count, five…four…three…still deeper, two…one…and zero. Now you step off at the bottom and will continue to go deeper and deeper with each breath you take, deeper and deeper with each breath, you are so relaxed and so comfortable. Let go still more, now I want you to make a suggestion to yourself that you want to carry out. You can stay in a trance while you decide what suggestion you want to make, deciding will be easy, it also will be easy for you to follow the suggestion whenever you wish to complete it. Go ahead now, and make your suggestion. Take whatever time you need, and after you have made your suggestion, you may arouse yourself from the trance at any time you wish and be wide awake and alert.

Confusion Induction Script

◆

This induction would be good for working with individuals who are highly intellectual people/critical thinkers.

Ask the client to take three long, slow deep breaths and then settle back comfortably with their eyes closed. Then begin with the following script;

Now, before you begin, I should say how glad I am to be working with you today, instead of a dull-witted mind, the kind you might find, in the gutter some place arguing with everyone, mad at the world, because when I see them, they keep shifting around, scratching itches, never getting comfortable, thinking they know it all, and no one can tell them what to do, not even to help them and they refuse to learn anything that might get them to climb out of that place and take care of themselves, so it is nice to know that anyone with your intelligence can easily learn how to drift into trance, so you can sit there, in that chair, here, while you try to be aware, of the exact meaning of the words you hear and all the changes that occur there in your thoughts, sensations, or awareness as I speak here, or you can forget to try to make the effort it takes to pay close attention to everything that happens, or does not happen in your experience, as you listen to me and also to your own thoughts, or to your sensations that change over time, or stay the same, in an arm or an ear, and your legs or fingers, and what about the thoughts, and the variety of images that speak to your mind's eye as I speak to your mind, and what you speak to yourself speaks for itself as you try to search and find that things may seem to be one thing, but turn out to be another, because two and two are four, but two can also mean also, and no two are alike, it all belongs to you and to your own ability to relax, those two ears too, and to begin to know, that you really don't know what means yes and what means no, here, though you may try to guess where you're going to go, you don't know that there is no real way to know how to let go while holding on and to recognize that there is nothing you need to try to know, to do, or not do, because everything you do allows you to recognize that I can say many different things and there is no need for you to make the effort it takes to try to make the effort to pay close attention to each thing I say, or don't say, because there was a time when the effort to train the mind to stay on track was not worth the trip that led the mind back to that time of peaceful, calm awareness, of effortless letting go, and knowing that you don't need to try to hear, or to understand what I might say later on here, the conscious mind, can go anywhere it wishes, while I continue to talk, and your conscious mind continues to hear, the way you overhear a conversation, you don't even need to do anything at all, it all belongs to you, as you begin to hear, the way you do, here and now, with your eyes closed, comfortable, that voice or sound in the background of the mind.

Piggyback Induction

◆

This induction method is for clients who have already experienced hypnotic trance. This procedure has the client revivifying their last hypnotic experience.

Ask the client to assume a comfortable position and start with their eyes closed. Read the following script:

As you continue to relax with your eyes closed, listening to the sound of my voice, you may begin to remember those experiences of hypnosis that you have had before, how it felt to listen to that voice speaking to you. Remembering that sound and the words…as you begin to drift down, that feeling in your hands or legs or arms, that feeling of relaxation perhaps, and what you thought as you begin to enter that deep state of trance, the sensations and images, the alterations in awareness, as your conscious mind became more and more comfortable, and your unconscious mind, assumed more and more responsibility for guiding and directing thoughts and responses, remembering where you were, in what position, what you did, what was said to you, how you felt as you learned to allow that trance to continue, and even now, as you continue to re-experience the memory of that event, and to allow those feelings to become a part of your experience now, I would like you to have the opportunity to enjoy allowing that trance to continue as you drift deeper and deeper, and my voice drifts with you, to become a part of your experience.

(Continue intervention).

Anxiety Script

◆

It is recommended to use this metaphor for clients with panic attacks and general anxiety.

Take the client to at least a medium state of trance and tell this story as you continue to pace their breathing.

It has been suggested, by a French physician that when babies are born, they should not be held upside down, in a cold, bright, noisy operating room, and spanked to make them cry, instead they should be born into a warm, quiet room with soft, gentle lights and put into a warm bath, because when they are treated that way, they open their eyes and look around, they seem amazed and happy, they even seem to smile, they lie there quietly relaxed, and they grow up to be happier and more secure, all because they were treated gently, protected and taken care of, not hurt or scared, but just allowed to be safe and quiet for a while, a natural way of doing things that seems to work out well, because almost all animals have their babies on warm spring nights when it is safe to be born, and the mother can take care of them, and help them get used to things, slowly and comfortably adjust to things, and learn how to keep things under control, they learn to hide quietly in the tall grass, how to remain very still, even when there is danger near, and they learn to play happily, secure in the awareness that someone is nearby, happen here, or the fun things that might occur later, because those old thoughts and fears aren't useful anymore, so you can relax and forget it, and go on about your business surprised to discover that you have been thinking about something else entirely, and you will know at that point, deep down in every cell in your body, that you won't have to feel that again, that it is over and done with, even more rapidly than you expected, not as soon as you would have liked, you can do it, now, and you can do it later, you can frighten yourself with that thought, or you can calmly relax yourself with a different thought, that's right, so practice and choose, it all belongs to you.

(Continue intervention or go to trance termination)

The Strawberry

◆

This script/metaphor is good for clients who are continually stressed out and need to learn to relax.

Take the client down in trance to a medium state and read this script as you pace their breathing pattern.

There is a delightful story I've heard, and I would like to share it with you, the story is about a young man who one day was walking through the forest, enjoying the beauty around him, as he walked he could hear the birds singing in the distance and hear the rustle of leaves under his feet as he walked along, feeling the shafts of warm sunlight as it filtered through the trees, what a glorious day it was, not a worry in the world, as he continued to walk he suddenly heard the rustle of leaves behind him, as he turned and looked, he saw that he was being stalked by a huge tiger, he began walking faster, and the tiger also started walking faster, the faster he walked the closer the tiger seemed to come, he seen a clearing in the forest in front of him, and decided to run for it, he started running very fast into the clearing, but too fast, at the edge of the clearing was a cliff, he ran so fast that he ran off the edge of the cliff, and as he started to fall, he reached out and grabbed hold of a tree root that was sticking out the side of the cliff, what a horrible situation to be in, he looked up to the top, because there was the tiger stalking back and forth waiting for him, he looked down and saw a river beneath him, but the were alligators in the river waiting for him to drop, if he went either up or down the cliff he was sure to be eaten by the animals, as he hung there by the tree root trying to decide what to do, he noticed that off to his right was a beautiful red wild strawberry growing, what a beautiful strawberry, it just glistened in the sunlight, what a wonderful strawberry red, he knew he had never seen such a perfect and pretty strawberry before in his life, he reached over and picked it, and held it in his fingers admiring how perfect and pretty it was.

(Continue the intervention or terminate trance)

Blue Sleep

◆

This is a short, direct script/metaphor for clients who suffer from insomnia.

Take the client into a medium state of trance and read this script as you pace their breathing pattern.

As you continue to relax, here is what you need to do, tonight and every night this week, as you lie down to go to sleep, and pray the lord your soul to keep, I want you to try to stay awake for at least one long hour, and during that time, I want you to think about nothing but blue, just let your thoughts fill with blue, and make sure you try to do that for an hour, before you finally let go, I know it will be difficult to experience nothing but the color blue, but I know you can do it for a while, so when my words come back to you, at night as you drift off to sleep, you will remember to try to stay awake, at least for a while, and to be aware of only blue, like the blue in the sky, or robin's egg blue, or the deep blue sea, a beautiful calm blue, remember to see only the color blue.

(Terminate trance)

The Journey of Learning

———————— ◆ ————————

After you have taken the client into trance slowly ready this metaphor while pacing their breathing.

Picture yourself walking slowly down the mountain, becoming more relaxed with each step you take. Each breeze that caresses your body relaxes you more and more. The path is made up of switchbacks, and each time you change direction you'll double your relaxation (Pause). You're about a third of the way down the mountain, enjoying every step, feeling a comfortable breeze blowing, keeping you not too hot and not too cool, but just right. you stop and look up at the clouds against a beautiful blue sky. Take a deep breath now, and peacefulness overtakes you and you continue down, deeper down the mountain. You've become more relaxed with each step that is taken, allowing every muscle in your face, neck and shoulders to let go of any tension. Your legs and feet feel great, walking down the mountain brings pleasure to your heart and body (Pause). You are halfway down the mountain, you see a place to stop and take a break, there is a tree and a stream and you are able to watch the birds fly about, taking some time to relax yourself deeper, deeper relaxed than you've been before (Pause). It is now time to journey to the bottom of the mountain and relax much more deeply now, down, down slowly deeper down the mountain in complete joy, peace, strength and energy. Nothing bothers you, nothing disturbs you in any way the peace that passes all understanding is yours. feelings of love and acceptance of who you are are yours. As you reach the bottom of the mountain you notice a fork in the path. You must make a decision which path to take. if you go to the left, you will experience your future with no changes. If you choose to go to the right, you can experience the changes you want to make now. first let us experience the left path, keeping all your behaviors, beliefs, and attitudes, see what your life is like for you now. What is it costing you physically, emotionally spiritually and financially? (Short pause) how do you feel? What do you say to yourself? (8 second pause) now go 5 years into the future. Look at yourself in the mirror, are you happy with what you see? (Short pause) What are your behaviors costing you? Financially, emotionally, socially and spiritually? (5-second pause). How do you feel about yourself? (Pause) What are you saying to yourself while you look into the mirror? (Pause) Now let's go ten years into the future. Look at yourself in the mirror, are you happy with what you see? (Pause) What are your behaviors costing you? Financially, emotionally, socially and spiritually? (Pause) How do you feel about yourself? (Pause) What are you saying to yourself while you look into the mirror? (Pause) Now I want you to go to the time when you're rocking in a rocking chair and reflecting on your whole life, what do you say to yourself? (Pause) What do you wish you had done differently? (Pause) What behaviors do you wish you had changed? What attitudes have hindered you? What beliefs about yourself and others have limited you? Is this the life you wanted? What learning can aid you back in the present? (Pause) Come back now to the crossroads and let's travel the path to the right. Take a couple of nice deep breaths, letting go. Now in your mind's eye experience yourself making the changes that are important to you. (Pause) Who you are tomorrow depends on the decisions you make today. Behaviors you want to change, beliefs about yourself that are limiting you. What new beliefs could you now believe about yourself and others? (Pause) What new attitudes can enhance your life? (Pause) now let's journey one year into your future, look in the mirror. See some of the positive changes that have taken place. How do you feel? (Pause) What do you say to yourself? (Pause) How have these changes affected you emotionally, socially, physically and financially? (Pause) What other areas in your life are different? (Pause) Now go five years into the future, look at yourself in the mirror, how happy are you with the changes you've made? (Pause) How have the changes affected you? (Pause) look into that mirror, what do you say to yourself? (Pause) Now go ten years into the future, look at yourself in the mirror, how happy are you with the changes you've made? (Pause) How have the changes affected you? (Pause) Look in to the mirror, what do you say to yourself? (Pause) Now go twenty years into the future, look at yourself in the mirror, how happy are you with the changes you've made? (Pause) How have the changes affected you? (Pause) Look in to the mirror, what do you say to yourself? (Pause) Now go fifty years into the future, look at yourself in the mirror, how happy are you now with the changes you have made? (Pause) How have these changes affected you? (Pause) Look into the mirror again, what do you say to yourself? (Pause) Now I want you to go to the time when you are rocking in a rocking chair, reflecting on your whole life. See how making one or two changes can make a difference on the outcome of your life. A change in a behavior, belief or attitude can have a rippling effect in many ways and in many areas of your life. How is your life richer financially? (Pause) How is your life richer spiritually? (Pause) What have been the benefits in terms of significant others, family, friends and others? (Pause) What other areas of your life have you improved? (Pause) Now what are you saying (use about eight second pauses) to yourself? (Pause) How do you feel about yourself knowing changes have taken place? (Pause) What is it like to look in the mirror at yourself? Enjoy it, intensify it! Come back to the present, today, and know that all of it is yours, the choices are yours, you have the ability to deal with (information gathered during the pre-talk). See yourself now dealing effectively with making the changes that you desire. Feel yourself being successful at what you set your mind to do.

(Continue Trance)

The View of Life

♦

The purpose of this exercise is to provide the individual and the therapist a better understanding of the individual and how they are oriented to life. This should provide significant insight for the individual into where they are in dealing with life and problems, and whether or not they chose to deal with them in therapy.

> Begin with taking the client down into trance, medium stage would be appropriate.
>
> Tell the client the following story: (Wherever you find a number in parenthesis, this denotes the recommended pause in seconds before moving on with the script)

Now I want you to picture yourself approaching a wall, this wall can be any size, shape, color or texture that you want it to be. Take time now to notice the wall. What does it look like? What does it feel like? Is it hot or cold? Does it have a smell? (12) Now you must cross the wall, you can use anything you want to cross to the other side, the only thing you can't do is blow-up the wall. (8) Now you find yourself in a nice forest setting, as you stroll down through the forest you can notice the tall trees and pretty flowers along the way. (4) Now you find yourself coming up to a river, you pause there to look at it. This can be a flow of water anywhere, because you have seen this flow of water before. (4) Now is the time for you to prepare for your journey up stream to the source of the water. You can take any thing you want with you on your journey to the source. (6) Now you have started your journey up stream in search of the source. (10) Now you are approaching the source of the water. (4) Now that you are at the source of the water, I want you to closely examine it. (6) Now its time for you to go back down stream. You slowly turn away from the source and start your journey back. (4) Along the way you notice a bit of a beach in front of you, I want you to stop there briefly now that you are on the beach doing whatever you want to do. (12) Now its time for you to leave the beach and continue back down stream. (4) As you continue back down stream you see the place where you started from. (4) Now you step back into the forest and walk back down the path until you see the wall again. (4) Now you are standing in front of the wall again, examine it closely now. (4) As before, you need to go to the other side of the wall now by any means you choose. (6) Now you are standing on the other side of the wall where your journey first begin.

Now bring the client back up from trance. Check their orientation to ensure that they are out of trance.

Explain the following meanings to them about what they encountered on their journey:

The first wall represents your natural wall of defenses to others in the world around you.

The forest represents nothing, a transition from the wall to the water.

The river/flow of water. This represents your flow of life as you are experiencing it presently.

The source of the river/flow of water represents your very life essence. Your source of energy, motivation, etc.

The beach, what you did on the beach represents your ability to play.

The second wall represents your present defenses in life.

Now have the client describe their journey in detail and assist them in understanding the significant points of their journey.

Low Self Esteem

Take the client to at least a Medium state of trance and read the following script while pacing the client's breathing.

Do you know of Beethoven, who became increasingly deaf as he got older, but kept on working, writing music that he could not hear, until one day, one evening, he conducted the symphony as they played his newest work, a concerto, and when it was finished the crowd erupted in applause, they stood and cheered, but he could not hear, he stood there facing the orchestra, unaware of the audience's approval until someone walked out and turned him around so he could see what he could not hear, only then did he know what everyone needs to know, but sometimes can't hear, like the woman I have heard of, black hair, black eyes, stocky build, a bright professional woman who hated herself and hated her life, she thought she was ugly and awful, and she thought that was why so many awful things had happened to her, but one day she was having lunch with a friend, an artist she had known for a time, and she said to her friend, that there were so many beautiful women, and they all seemed to be on that street that day, and her friend simply said, I think you're the most beautiful woman I've ever seen, and went on eating, as if it were nothing, and that simple observation, that simply statement of opinion, matter of fact, not flattery, wouldn't go away, couldn't be undone, her friend was an artist who knew what beauty was, so she could not ignore it, and she could not forget it, instead she begin to look at herself, each day in the mirror, and she began to look at others, how they looked, who they were with, and it was very hard and scary at first to realize how wrong she had been, how wrong her mother had been, how wrong she had been about herself in so many different ways, but over time she had began to accept it, she was not ugly, she was not stupid, she was not a bad person, she was attractive and likeable and nice, and she did not have to settle for less than she deserved, how she thought changed, how she felt changed, what she did changed, her life changed, all because of one brief comment, one brief glimpse of herself, a clear admission of something she had been unable to let herself know before, that truth is beauty and beauty truth, and the truth about oneself, one's beauty is in the eye of the beholder, but what we hear is not always measured on a hearing test, Beethoven heard things in his mind that his ears could no longer hear, and many animals can hear sounds that the human ear cannot, and all we ever need to hear is that there is nothing else we need to do, except hear the beauty of what is.

(Terminate Trance)

Wonderland

◆

This script/metaphor is for helping clients with their self-perception or self-esteem.

Take the client into a medium state of trance and read the story while pacing their breathing pattern.

While you continue to relax, I can wonder how Alice in wonderland felt as she met all those unusual creatures and heard all those strange words, but kept going on her way not knowing what to expect that day, not knowing what was next or where to go, might seem to be strange at first, but after a while it becomes an adventure that delights the child and fascinates the mind, because you never do know what's next, what will be, but you can know that it is okay not to know what the future holds in store, because things change over time and things change in the mind, as your unconscious mind changes your mind about how things feel and are, like Alice when she saw that bottle that said, drink me on the label, and when she did, she got larger, then smaller than she had ever been before, or at least it seemed that way to her, and it may be interesting to notice that when people relax things begin to change, one arm may seem higher than the other, or a leg may seem heavier than before, and even the entire body becomes more difficult to find, it may seem to float at times or to get smaller and smaller, as the chair feels bigger and bigger, or the feet seem to change in some way, while the hands do it differently, and after a while you begin to wonder how you'll ever pull it all back together just the way it belongs, but how does it belong, really, and what is the way it should be, because taste changes over time, so what we prefer today is not what we'll want tomorrow, and what seems to be exactly right now may be what is left over later on, and every where you look, things are changing, rearranging, so it is hard to know what is the way things ought to be, in summer, trees are in full bloom, though their flowers are no longer there, and in autumn the green changes, becomes reds, oranges, browns and yellows, and in winter they're all gone, and begin again next spring, only now a new limb grows here, and an old one dies there, and how should that tree be, taller or shorter, more leaves or fewer, greener or rounder perhaps, though there are those who might say that the tree is just the way it is, and the way it is, is all it needs to be, the way they see a newborn child, each tiny finger exactly perfect, each tiny ear perfectly exact, though no two look the same, like Alice in Wonderland, where everything seems different, and she discovered how it felt to love being just what she was.

(Continue with intervention or terminate trance)

Self Esteem

This is a good short-term approach to raising your client's self-esteem. It is fast, effective and repeatable.

Take client down in trance, Medium to Somnambulism, read the script while pacing the client's breathing throughout the trance experience.

It is easy to pay close attention to things that are wrong, it's easy to be a critic, to find fault with everything, it's easy to not like yourself, or to not trust yourself to be ok it's harder to have the courage to see things in a different light, it's harder to take a risk and to enjoy yourself, your life, and other people, it's easy to find reasons to not feel good, to not feel comfortable, to hide from oneself and others, it's harder to say what the heck, to not care what anyone thinks, it's hard to give yourself permission to feel good no matter what, or is it? Maybe it's easy, maybe it's easy to do, but you have been afraid to do it, because you do know how, and you can do it now, but sometimes it feels wrong to really believe you're o.k, when you might be wrong, but who's to say, and so from now on, I want you to know it's ok to do that crazy thing, to let yourself feel that way, you can do it now, today, and you can do it tomorrow, you can see what's okay about you and what you do, you can see those things quite clearly, and feel quite comfortable too, you can alter your mind and alter your mood, even if you have to pretend for a while, that this new way of thinking and feeling is because of something you took or something that was done to you and you can't really help it, that's just the way you feel, confident, happy and pleased, it's good to know that you control that feeling, until that feeling becomes real, so do it now, or just let your unconscious mind do it for you, so you don't have to know what's gotten into you when your whole way of thinking about you changes.

(Terminate trance)

Adjusting Your Thermostat

◆

This script/metaphor will help the client gain better self-acceptance of themselves and their situations.

Take the client down in trance to a medium state and read the script while pacing their breathing pattern.

We all have come to enjoy the luxury of being able to have a warm room in the winter and a cool room when its hot outside, and to be able to set a thermostat that maintains a constant temperature, no matter how much the weather changes, now we have computer controlled devices that turn off the furnace after we leave, turn it back on when we come home, and turn it down again at night, when we are snuggled under the covers, all quite automatically, but all you have to do is look around the world to see that things were not always so, because up north where they have winters they have learned to use the cold to create winter sports people down south have never seen, and even their clothes are different, warmer and more weatherproof, because they know they can't change the cold, so they use it for all its worth, while people in the south have their own styles and their own sports, and in the really hot spots they barely wear any clothes at all, and sometimes they don't do anything at all, because they know that if you can't change it, you'd better not fight it, and you might as well use it, so everywhere you go, even though we can control it inside, we still can't control it outside, and if its not quite right inside, you can make it warmer or cooler, but if its not quite right outside, then you might as well make the most of it and use it to your own advantage and get used to it and even like it like that because that's how it is, and it is always more pleasant to want what you've got and to learn to enjoy it, unless you decide to move some place else, which some people can't do, and other people wouldn't do if they could, because they feel at home there, like they belong there exactly where they are, whether the weather is too hot or so cold it freezes fire, they like it like that and they have found some way to take full advantage of just the way it is, the way movie stars do, because they come in all sizes and shapes, with every size nose and ear and eyes, which they learn to use to their full advantage, their own unique quality, their own special appeal that they amplify and enjoy in much the same way you do, enjoying what others enjoy, because they've learned to enjoy exactly what they have, so we do Too.

(Proceed with intervention or go to trance termination)

Your Museum

◆

This script/metaphor is good for clients to learn and accept their own uniqueness as an individual.

Take client down in trance to a medium state and begin reading the script as you continue pacing their breathing.

As you have already guessed, there is no perfect way to relax or to enter into trance, because it happens naturally, it is always different each time, no two snowflakes are exactly alike, and even the fingerprints of twins differ, so who's to say which one is the right one, and which one is the left, and no matter how hard we try to do things perfectly, the odd thing is we always prefer the thing that is different and unique, something that is one of a kind, like stamps printed upside down, or coins made a little bit wrong, those become prized collector's items, just because they are different from all the rest, even if you need a magnifying lens to see the imperfection, because we want to see things differently, to see things bigger or smaller than we think they are, like a mirror in a circus that changes our shape and form, so we can really see what different would be if different we really were, which may explain the collections in art museums around the world, on one wall is a Van Gogh, on another is a Picasso, their beauty and power stands out, but everything is out of place or out of proportion, two legs different lengths or two arms different sizes, and yet it is all art of the highest form, the different paintings, different styles, like clothing styles that change from one age to another, and yet each is beautiful and flattering in its own way, in the eye of the beholder every flower is unique, designed the way it should be to be exactly what it is, and that is why we used to play a game of sorts as children, to decide which flower we would be and which we already were, and then to really look at it later and be surprised by what we found, something you can do as well, whenever you decide which flower you belong to, but for right now we don't need to know how you will feel when you decide to know that what seems wrong can be quite right after all, after you do all your homework and explore your own museum in the gardens of your mind where you can collect what you need to know to protect your own treasure and to treasure what you have collected even after you think you know that you really do not know what they really think about what you think about you.

(Continue with intervention or terminate trance)

Fail Safe Script

♦

This metaphor script is useful for clients with fear of failure and test anxiety.

Take the client down in trance to a medium state and read this story pacing their breathing.

Because everyone needs to relax at times, even Olympic athletes who are under great pressure to perform, and sometimes must be perfect to win, needs some way to relax, and to put things into perspective, to recognize that it is just a sport and not a war between nations, because a war is one thing and a game is something else entirely, especially in this atomic age where a war could mean the end of everything, we really cannot afford to make even the smallest of mistakes, and so some people are terrified that the failsafe system will fail, and that will be the end of it all, all because of some tiny little error, somebody doing something wrong or saying the wrong thing at the wrong time in the wrong way to the wrong person, and everything goes up in flames, which is why they have special programs, for the people working with those systems, because what they have to do is so dangerous and so terribly important that special training and counseling is required, the only place in the world, perhaps, where mistakes can not be allowed, and it is comforting to note that almost everyplace else, an error is just an opportunity to do it differently later on, because perfection is rarely required and perfection is seldom needed and even the Olympic athletes are never perfect all the time, and sometimes do things wrong like the Navahos when they weave a rug, who always leave a knot, an imperfection, so the gods won't be angered, and think they are trying to be gods themselves, but that is another story, about what is really important, and what is not, and how it feels to give permission to enjoy the feelings of the freedom to feel safe doing these things, knowing that the world won't end, if you leave a knot some place, so the gods can relax, knowing you are not challenging them, just doing the best you can, letting it go at that.

(Continue with intervention or terminate trance)

Craving Again

◆

This script/metaphor is best used with a client who still experiences and urge or craving for a substance they have withdrawn from.

Take the client into a medium state of trance and proceed to read this script while pacing their breathing pattern.

This is a story about a person named Marsha, wedding bells in Marsha's future were not something that she was looking forward to, and it wasn't just because it wasn't her own wedding, it didn't matter who was getting married, it was going to be a big problem for her, she was just newly recovered from active alcoholism and very frightened about her urges and her wanting to drink, and when ever she would have an urge and a thought about how really fun it would be to drink, she began worrying, consumed by the thought she would find herself drinking, and she really had that experience that people have whenever you want to change some kind of behavior and move two steps forward and one back, and having doubts whenever you think about engaging in that new behavior, and it was only a few days before she was going to find herself in that very difficult situation, any person who is working on recovery knows that wedding receptions can be one of the most difficult tests, with everybody drinking and engaging in that behavior that you're trying to stop, fear, concern and apprehension were written all over her face when I saw her for therapy that day, she had good reason to be apprehensive too, the odds of her staying away from using were slim, she thought about drinking a lot and it didn't seem that she had the resources to avoid the temptation since she was so new at recovering, she was nothing like Jane who had just canceled her scheduled appointment with me, Jane had a great deal more experience with sobriety than Marsha, and also a lot more confidence, with good reason, some people might have said she was a little cocky, but she had good reason to be really confident of her ability to stay sober, she never really had urges and didn't have to go through the changes and the struggles like Marsha had to do to stay sober, and Jane was even so confident that she was able to go to parties and not even want to drink, that was such a positive sign to a lot of people because when you can be around users and not want to use, it can be a good indication that chemicals are not such a major focus in your life. Well, Marsha's reception and Jane's party were obviously going to be two very different experiences, I only wished that Marsha could have had some of Jane's confidence, she really could have used it, but unfortunately, she didn't, and I knew that next week's therapy would involve a lot of processing with Marsha, regarding her relapse and attempting to develop some ways for her to do a better job next time, for each time you make a mistake in a behavior change, you can learn from that, I'm sure there are many experiences that, even if you don't consciously recall the times when you've made mistakes and failed at things, you've been able to learn from them, you can unconsciously know that, and unconsciously recall those experiences, and I also look forward to being able to celebrate Jane's pride at being able to once again not relapse in a tough situation, if she chanced to keep her appointment at all next week, so I was really quite surprised when I got a chance to celebrate Marsha's successful reception and process Jane's relapse, perhaps you have some ideas as to how Marsha was able to use her situation in a useful way, and now Jane was unable to do that which she thought she would find so easy, and I was, of course, interested too, and I asked Marsha how she was able to have those feelings that were so scary for her, and yet act in a way that was totally opposite of those feelings, and act in a way that was so useful to her, basically, what she said was that she was able to take those actions which are most useful, and for her it was to seek out those people at the reception who were supportive of not drinking, or to find herself intrigued with something else, several people had come from another country, and how interesting it was to learn about that culture, and she said that she had learned to use her fear and urges as a barometer that indicated that there were things that she needed to change, and so each time in the future that she was to have those fears or urges, that was her signal that it was time to do some new things, Jane had some learning too, later that can become evident, balancing confidence with over confidence is important in any behavior, the athlete who has no confidence will never enter the race, the athlete who is over confident may not train hard enough, I'm not sure what Jane thought she had learned, just imagine that you're not really sure exactly what you're going to be learning later about it, on a conscious level, some learning are real obvious, but unconsciously those applications can be used in many different ways, and so you simply apply those unconscious learning, and perhaps delight yourself in how you are able to later surprise, and maybe impress yourself in exactly how you're able to apply that.

Balloon Technique

◆

This technique can be used for intervention with various problems; i.e., Grieving, Stop Smoking and Habit Control.

During the assessment interview note the significant points that stop a person from achieving the desired change.

Take the client into trance, deepen to somnambulism.

Ask the client to go to their special place, a place that they feel comfortable, safe and secure. Build the intensity of their special place.

Sample script/example for stop smoking and the significant points to overcome are as an example;

(1) Craving tobacco
(2) Light headiness
(3) Unspecified anxiety.

Enjoying your special place, knowing that you are comfortable and safe there, notice the colors about your special place, how very nice, notice all the other things about your special place, the sights, the sounds, the colors, no one else can be in your special place unless you allow them, what a wonderful place to be, so comfortable and safe in your special place, so wonderful, notice how you feel, comfortable and safe, enjoying your special place. Notice that in your (left) (right) hand you are holding three balloons, three of the ugliest balloons you have ever seen in your life, these ugly balloons look so out of place in your special place, these are such ugly repulsive colors on these balloons. The first balloon has the words, "Craving tobacco" wrote on the side, the words are clear and easy to read, the second ugly balloon has the words "Light headiness" clearly printed on the side, the third ugly balloon has the word "Anxiety" clearly on the side. There you stand with these three very ugly balloons with the words, "Craving tobacco", "Light headiness" and "Anxiety" wrote on the balloons. These ugly balloons certainly do not belong in your special place, as you observe these ugly balloons with the words on them, you realize even more that they don't belong in your special, beautiful place. When you are ready, you can release these ugly balloons and watch them slowly float up and away, moving slowly out of sight, As the balloons start to fade away, so does the words printed on them, remembering briefly that the words were "Craving tobacco", "Light heartiness" and "Anxiety". Watch them slowly disappear from sight (Pause). Now you can see yourself in your special place, free of the ugly balloons, free of the tobacco craving, light heartiness and anxiety, seeing yourself in your special place as a non smoker, noticing how you look now, how wonderful, notice how very wonderful you feel, feeling so proud of yourself now that you are a non-smoker, how wonderful to be so rightfully proud of yourself, seeing yourself as a non smoker, experiencing how it feels to be a non smoker, how wonderful. Continue to relax, perhaps moving even one level deeper, enjoying the experience of being a non-smoker.

(Bring client out of trance and process the experience)

Smoking Abstinence Script

◆

Take the client down to a medium state of trance and read the script while pacing their breathing pattern.

Now many people have come to me and asked for help with some particular difficulty, and they say to me, "I have no motivation, I have no discipline", and I say to them, "The unmotivated person doesn't call for an appointment. The undisciplined person doesn't show up on time". The unmotivated person does not distinguish the place they wish to be, from the place where they are now. The undisciplined person stays home. Now you have all the motivation you need. You have all the discipline you need, though there is one thing you still need which you don't have yet, and that's self-confidence, the self-confidence it takes to set out on a journey completely prepared for the trip, knowing you've read the map, you've charted the course, reservations taken care of, believing you can, will, reach your destination quickly, easily, effortlessly. The self-confidence it takes to recognize all the signs of success. Just as now, you recognize those comfortable hypnotic sensations in the hands, arms, legs, those physical signs that allow you to know you've traveled from one state to another state in a calm, confident way, and you can offer yourself large portions of self-confidence, large portions of self-esteem, you can breathe in self-confidence and breathe out self doubt as you continue to enjoy the journey towards your goal. Throughout the years that I have worked with people who have had many problems. They have become obsessed with the idea of making love with someone they are attracted to, and when they have raised the subject with the object of their desire they've been told, in no uncertain terms, that a physical relationship was an impossibility, and the reasons given for the impossibility has been many. It is dangerous or risky, unhealthy or even unethical, and yet, faced with all these obstacles, these clients become more and more obsessed, convinced that their happiness depends on the consummation of their desires, to the neglect of all other aspects of their lives. Which reminds me of the man who had just bought a brand new house, an expensive house, in the nicest part of town, he had admired that house for many, many years, maybe since he was a teenager, maybe from his twenties, he couldn't remember exactly, but he did know he'd been wanting to buy that house for a long, long time, and now here it was. He lavished care and attention on it, decorated it in tasteful colors of (Insert color of client's clothing). He papered and painted and hardly paid any attention at all to that growing headache at first, in fact it was several years before he noticed that his head seemed to have a continual dull ache, and his muscles were aching as well, he felt tired a lot too, so he visited a doctor who gave him a prescription, but he just never felt much better and everything failed to stop that headache, or the irritation and the insidious feeling that his health was fading away, but at least he had his house, and it is easy to understand how he might feel if you've ever gone from house to house, real estate open houses perhaps, or just going to someone else's home, seeing how the other half lives can be an educational experience, but I can understand my client's obsession with something that's not about to happen, from the day I saw my dream house, of course the price was very beyond what I could possibly afford, and yet I couldn't get it out of my mind, I imagined myself in the living room, in the den, and was certain I must have it to be happy. Now everybody knows that nobody likes to be told what to do, and if I could tell you what to do you wouldn't have to be here today. You'd call me on the phone, and you'd say, "I'd like to quit smoking", and I would say, "That's a wonderful idea, quit smoking…now". but everybody knows nobody likes to be told what to do, so I won't say to you, you already know all the reasons for ending this smoking problem, I wouldn't have to say to you that smoking is dangerous and unhealthy…I wouldn't have to tell you that you will receive no pleasure from smoking, I never need to say that cigarettes are a poor substitute for (insert client's rational for smoking) but one thing I will say to you is: "Not smoking is not a task you wouldn't find easy". When you leave here today you'll no longer be somebody who smokes, you know you have the desire to smoke, and you know you know it, and no one can talk you out of it, but what you know now that you didn't know before, is you also have a large amount of no desire, and you can get to know this place of no desire as it expands and grows larger and larger, and the feeling of no desire can reach deeper and deeper, the time of no desire continues to lengthen, and no way is easier than this, and I read once when I was a child, I thought like a child, I acted like a child. Now that I am grown I have put away the things of childhood, what does that really mean? I'm not sure, but it certainly meant a lot to clients who were obsessed with a sexual desire that could never be fulfilled. Perhaps it was the thought of putting old ways behind them that finally allowed them to be free, or perhaps they simply grew up and took responsibility for their feelings and their behavior. Disappointment is something we all face from time to time, and you can imagine how disappointed that man was to learn there was insecticide in the floor and walls of that house. He went on his dream vacation, and was amazed to discover his headaches and sickness disappeared in just a few days time. When he got home he contacted an expert and the expert gently broke the news, his entire house was slowly being poisoned, and so was he. It only took him one day to pack his things. He knew for certain his health was worth more than any house, no matter how long he'd wanted it, and I guess I finally came to terms with the fact that he couldn't buy a $300,000 home, no matter what he did. It was a nice dream, but the price was to high to pay, especially since there was no Jacuzzi and it is good to finally resolve those feelings and to just let go, not needing to now how the unconscious mind knows what to do. For you, thinking with an awareness of things thought, without needing to know those things which will get done automatically, you know what, to do, now I would prefer you stop smoking immediately, but its entirely up to you to discover today the best time and way for you. Some clients wait an hour, some wait until after dinner, some stop entirely right before bed. Now, I would prefer you stop immediately, but its completely up to you to choose the time, a time today, when you free yourself from smoking forever.

(Continue with intervention or terminate trance)

Blended Technique for Stop Smoking

◆

Before putting the client in trance, start with the following script and follow through. Ensure that the client's answers are stated in the positive. Do not accept an answer of don't know.

What is your motivation to stop smoking?
Why do you want to stop?
Is it for yourself or someone else?
When did you start smoking?
What family members smoke?
What is the quality of the relationship with those people?
What is most stressful to you?
What is fun for you?
What situations in the past prompted you to smoke?
Where are you when you smoke?
What are you doing when you smoke?
What one word signifies to you complete relaxation?

I want you to now think of that word in your mind and touch your thumb and your index finger together. From now on each time you want to completely relax and use self-hypnosis, go ahead and use this technique.

Now, take two deep breaths and use this technique and relax. Initiate trance induction, install ideomotor signaling. Have the client do the arm lift test to verify trance depth. "I want you to become aware of the part of your subconscious that allows you to smoke (Pause). If that part of your subconscious does not object, I would like to communicate with that part. Please have that part of your subconscious signify it is ok by raising the index finger on your right hand if it is not ok. Please lift the index finger on your left hand. (Thank the part) I would like to now communicate with the part of your subconscious that allows you to smoke and find out what the payoff for smoking is. I know that it is used as a positive tool". (Pause) If the subconscious has problems finding one give examples such as stress, socialize, gratification, to feel good, friends. "I would now like the subconscious part to generate at least three new healthy alternatives to smoking (Pause). Identify with someone who you admire and does not smoke". When alternatives are found ask the subconscious if these alternatives are acceptable and do they seem and feel acceptable? If no, go back to the unconscious and identify new alternatives that would be acceptable. Now for this next intervention I will need your permission to touch your shoulder. I want you to allow your mind to go to your favorite place to smoke, where you experience all the feelings and gratifications you get when you smoke (Pause). Now let your mind go to a time when you knew you were in complete control of a situation. You had all the answers and every thing you did was right (Pause). Imagine that you are experiencing it again. Pay attention to all you saw, felt, and words that you heard and the way you talked to yourself. (Pause). When you see that the person has achieved this touch their shoulder for 15 seconds. "I want you to now drift back to your favorite situation in which you liked to smoke and to experience being in control again of this situation and say no" (Pause). When the client acknowledges they have said no, touch them again on the shoulder for 15 seconds. "I would like you to imagine a situation that occurs two weeks from now when you would have smoked. How does it feel to be a non-smoker? Your subconscious has all the tools you'll need. It has all the dials to tune in whatever is nice for you and to tune out what you don't need to hear or listen to. Your subconscious has

so much data, everything you have seen and heard and felt in your life is stored there. It is all there just as data to put together for whatever new ways of perceiving and experiencing that will help you to stop smoking".
(Terminate trance)

Dogs

◆

This script/metaphor is good for clients who have a problem with procrastination.

Take the client down in trance to a medium state and read this script while pacing their breathing.

You can relax completely and I can explain to your unconscious mind a story I heard from a friend who has a friend whose son was in school at a distant university, he was failing his courses because he would not go to class, and he would not do his homework, though he said he wanted to, so he went to see a counselor who told him to drop out of school, and to raise dogs or lions, because they would growl and attack, if he didn't take care of his business, this put him off at first, made him angry, so angry he just did it, went to class, did his homework, got all A's, and each time he found it hard, to do what he needed to do, he thought about raising puppies, and all he would have to go through with their little piles here and there, as they did just what they wanted to do, whenever and wherever they wanted, though he did know from experience, that even a tiny puppy can eventually be trained to behave its self, even if its hard to do, what it really doesn't want to do, to wait and do it in the right place at the right time, because who would want to live with it, if it never did learn to behave itself and to stop acting like a spoiled soiling pup, and so even the most rebellious pup has a

willingness to take care of itself, and self worth, the young man learned his lesson.
 (Terminate)

Bandits

◆

This script/metaphor is useful for clients who have a problem with procrastination.

Take the client down in trance to a medium state and read the script while pacing their breathing pattern.

I want to share a story with you about two cowboys who became bandits, they decided to become bank robbers, they thought that would provide them with a great deal of money, they had trouble deciding which town in South Texas they would rob their first bank in, after weeks of discussing which town, they finally gave up, and decided to rob the bank of the town they were already in, the cowboys entered the bank the following month, and proceeded to rob it, as they ran from the bank and jumped on their horses the alarm was sounded, as they rode out of town there was already a posse being formed to chase them, they rode hard and fast towards Old Mexico to gain safety, when they reached the Rio Grand River, the found that the river was high and flooding its banks, so they must change directions, to the east was mountains, but they couldn't decide, they were fearful of freezing to death in the mountains, to the west was a desert, they couldn't decide, they were fearful they would die of thirst in the desert, to the north the posse was coming after them, they couldn't go that way, for fear the posse would shoot them to death or hang them, what were they to do, they just couldn't seem to decide, so they sat down and died.

(Terminate trance)

Chronic Pain Management

◆

Applications: Long term pain, back injuries, nerve damage, phantom limb pain, cancer.

Induce trance to somnambulism, read script pacing the client's breathing pattern.

With your eyes closed, as you begin to relax, you probably notice that the first thing you notice is how difficult it is to not become aware of that pain and discomfort, and that's fine, you don't need to fight your mind which is always aware of those sensations there for you, because as you relax, you can begin to discover that each time you relax a muscle in your arm…or a leg…or your face…or even a foot…or a finger, that you can drift down more and more deeply than before, into that sensation there in a more relaxed and comfortable way, because there really is no need to make the effort it takes to try to stay away from that feeling or to try to fight that feeling, which almost seems to guide and direct awareness down toward it, more and more into it, and as you drift toward it, toward that center of that feeling, everything else can be allowed to relax, to relax more and more, as you begin to discover that it really is ok to let go in that way, to allow yourself to relax every other part of your body and to drift down toward the very tiniest center of that feeling, the very small middle of it, the source of it, and then to drift down through that center into a place, just as that drifting upwards occurs as well, a drifting back toward the surface of wakeful awareness, as your unconscious mind reminds you to drift up in a relaxed, comfortable way, back towards the surface now, bring with you that comfortable relaxation, that automatic change in sensation, even as the mind drifts upwards, the relaxation continues, as the mind awakens and the eyes open, but the body remains behind, relaxed, that's right, eyes open now (pause) but before you come back completely, you can close those eyes again, and feel that relaxation again, and recognize that ability, that ability to relax, to let your unconscious mind find the way to provide you with more and more comfort, more and more relaxed, letting go, that's right, aware that you can do so, anytime, anyplace you need or want to, you can return to that place, so here is what you do, later on today, tomorrow, next week, and for the rest of your life, whenever you need to or want to, you can close your eyes just for a moment, perhaps, and feel that comfortable feeling, that change in sensation, returns to you, and you drift into that light trance, or a deep trance, where your unconscious mind can take care of you, make things comfortable for you, and then you return to the surface of wakeful awareness, not needing to make the effort it takes to try to tell if that feeling is there or not, just as you return now back to the surface, comfortably relaxed and refreshed, remaining relaxed.

Long Term Pain Management

◆

Applications are for long term pain, back injuries, nerve damage, phantom limb pain, and cancer.

Induce trance and read the script pacing the client's breathing pattern throughout trance.

As you relax, you probably notice that the first thing you notice is how difficult it is to not become aware of that pain and discomfort, and that's fine, you don't need to fight your mind which is always aware of those feelings there for you, because as you relax, you can begin to discover that each time you relax a muscle in your arm…or a leg…or your face…or even a foot…or a finger, that you can drift down more and more deeply than before, into that feeling there in a more relaxed and comfortable way, because there really is no need to make the effort it takes to try to stay away from that feeling or to try to fight that feeling, which almost seems to guide and direct awareness down toward it, more and more into it, and as you drift toward it, toward that center of that feeling, everything else can be allowed to relax, to relax more and more, as you begin to discover that it really is ok to let go in that way, to allow yourself to relax every other part of your body and to drift down toward the very tiniest center of that feeling, the very small middle of it, the source of it, and then to drift down through that center into a place beneath it of quietness and calm awareness, down through that feeling, and out the other side, into a space of relaxed letting go, of comfortable relaxation, where the mind can drift, the way waves drift from one place to another as that body relaxes and the mind becomes smoother and smoother, able to absorb events, even those events, easily and comfortably, to become absorbed in thoughts and images, as the mind reflects the clear wonder of a child, a young child, watching a flock of geese as they soar across the sky and fly into the clouds, the rhythm of their sound becoming softer and softer, as soft as the down in a pillow in a place where you rest and relax, a most comfortable place for a child to relax and drift into dreams through the mind, protected and safe, where the letting go allows the flow and the soft floating upwards, where the mind drifts free of things far below, and seems to soar in a sky as clear as glass, so smooth and clear that it disappears when you look into it, and what appears instead is the deep blue shine of the warm soft sun, a star far beyond that reaches out and provides that warm soft light as you drift down and experience the comfort and learn to feel the sound sleep that your unconscious mind can provide you whenever you relax and allow it to drift into a trance, because it can take you down through that feeling, into a space, that relaxed comfortable place, as you relax and allow it to do so just for you, that relief and relaxation, that drifting down through which comes to you whenever you allow it to, just as that drifting upwards occurs as well, a drifting back toward the surface of wakeful awareness, as your unconscious mind reminds you to drift up in a relaxed, comfortable way, back towards the surface now, bring with you that comfortable relaxation, that automatic change in feeling, even as the mind drifts upwards, the relaxation continues, as the mind awakens and the eyes open, but the body remains behind, relaxed, that's right, eyes open now (Pause) but before you come back completely, you can close those eyes again, and feel that relaxation again, (pause) and recognize that ability, that ability to relax, to let your unconscious mind find the way to provide you with more and more comfort, more and more relaxed, letting go, that's right, aware that you can do so, anytime, anyplace you need or want to, you can return to that place, so here is what you do, later on today, tomorrow, next week, and for the rest of your life, whenever you need to or want to, you can close your eyes just for a moment, perhaps, and feel that comfortable feeling, that change in sensation, returns to you, and you drift into that light trance, or a deep trance, where your unconscious mind can take care of you, make things comfortable for you, and then you return to the surface of wakeful awareness, not needing to make the effort it takes to try to tell if that feeling is there or not, just as you return now back to the surface, comfortably rested and refreshed, remaining relaxed perhaps, even as the eyes open again.

(Terminate trance)

Transient (Brief) Pain Management

◆

Applications; Dental work, surgery, sports injuries, sprains, headaches, child birthing, Induce trance and read the script pacing client's breathing pattern throughout the trance work.

You are sitting there comfortably aware that you have come here today because you want to gain control of your own abilities, to eliminate some future feelings of discomfort, and as you continue to relax and to drift down into a deep trance, I want you to take your time, not too fast, not too slow, because there are some things you need to listen to carefully, first you need to understand that you already have the ability to lose an arm or a hand, to become completely unaware of exactly where that arm is positioned, or what it is doing, and you have the ability to be not concerned about exactly where that arm is, or that hand or leg, or your entire body for that fact, this may seem to take too much effort to pay attention to at times, because you also have an unconscious ability you can learn how to use effectively, and that ability is to turn off the feeling in an arm, a leg, or anywhere you choose, and once you discover how it feels to not feel anything at all, wherever you want that to occur, then you can create the numb, comfortable feeling, anywhere, Any time it is useful to you, and I don't know whether your unconscious mind will allow you to discover that numb feeling in the right hand, or a finger of the left hand first, a tiny area of numbness, a comfortable tingling feeling, a heavy thick numbness, that seems to grow and spreads over time, until it covers that hand, the back of the hand, or anything else you pay close attention to, it's your choice, it just seems to disappear from your experience, but you don't know how it feels, to not feel something that isn't there, so here is what I want you to do, I want you to reach over to that numb area, to that numb hand, that's right, go ahead and touch it, (Pause), and feel that touching as you begin to pinch yourself there, at first you may experience a feeling, but as you continue to pinch yourself, an interesting thing happens (slight pause) you begin to discover that there are times when you feel nothing at all there, that's right, the feeling just seems to disappear, as you continue to learn how to allow your unconscious mind to turn off those feelings, all you need to do is just pay very close attention to the numbness, and as that ability grows and develops, and you begin to know, really know beyond a doubt, that you already do know how to allow feeling and pain to disappear from your hand, or anywhere, your other hand can return to a resting place of its choice, and you can drift up to that point where wakeful awareness will return, so go ahead now, as you relax, and discover how to let go and to feel that numbness more and more clearly, and you can drift up more, in your own time, in your own comfortable way, that's right, take your time to learn, and then drifting back upwards, eyes opening (pause) now, before you wake up completely, I would like you to close your eyes again, and allow that drifting down again, reentering that place of calm relaxation, perhaps going even deeper than before, while you drift down again, there is a story I want to tell you about a young boy on TV not long ago in the past, he had learned to control all of his pain, he described the steps he went down in his mind, one at a time down those steps, until he found this hall at the bottom, like a long tunnel, and all along the tunnel on both sides were many different switches, switchboxes, each clearly labeled, one for the right hand, one for the left, one for the leg, and one for every place on the body, and he could see the wires to those switches clearly, the nerves that carried the feelings from one place to another, all going through those switches and switchboxes, all he needed to do was to reach up in his mind and turn off the switches he wanted to, and then he could feel nothing at all, no feelings could get through from there, no feelings at all, because he had turned off those switches, he used his mind's abilities differently from the man who simply made his body numb, he didn't know how he did it exactly, all he knew was he relaxed and disconnected, like a train car disconnecting from the rest, moved his mind away from his body, moving it outside some place else, where he could watch and listen, but drift off some place else, and it really doesn't matter exactly how you tell your unconscious what to do, or how your unconscious does it for you, the only thing of importance is that you know you can lose the feelings as easily as closing your eyes, and drifting down within, where something unknown in the unconscious happens that allows you to disconnect from the uncomfortable feeling, that allows that numbness to occur…And then a drifting upwards now, upwards towards the surface and slowly allowing the eyes to open as wakeful awareness returns with a comfortable continuation of that protected feeling of safe, secure relaxation and an ability to forget an arm, or anything at all, with no need to pay attention to things that are just fine, that somebody else can take care of while you drift in your mind, remaining secure in this new knowledge you have gained (Pause), now it is time to enjoy that comfortable drifting upwards where the eyes open, and wakeful awareness returns quite completely now.

(Terminate trance)

Ulcer and Colitis Script

◆

Use this in trance when the client is deepened to a medium state, always pacing the breathing during trance.

Everyone is familiar with Smokey the Bear, and his pleas with campers to make sure their fires are completely out, so every scout learns how to put fires out, to make sure everything is cool, nothing left smoldering or hot, by pouring water on it, or dumping snow on it, just the way you're suppose to, keeping it cool while relaxing in the shade drinking a tall glass of ice water and watching that coolness spread, making sure it's completely out so you can leave the woods feeling relaxed and calm knowing nothing will catch and spread, because fire is to hot to handle unless you wear special gloves, insulated and made of fireproof materials which used to be very thick and heavy, but now there is a new material coated with a very thin layer of metal which is shiny and reflects all the heat, and keeps everything cool, even down to absolute zero, which is as cold as things can get, but they cool off nuclear reactors in a very different way, because when a reactor gets hot it means there are to many electrons flying around inside, so they lower in carbon rods that absorbs those electrons, absorbs all that energy, and as things quiet down, they also cool off, like turning off a spigot to quiet that dripping sound, shutting off the valve that stops the flow in there, they can also coat the walls with something cool and thick, like they do in houses, to insulate and protect, to keep the people inside comfortable in any weather, the way skin protects us from many things, but when it gets cut or scratched it needs to grow back together to heal that tiny hole, and so we take care of it, put a band-aide over it, and are careful not to bump it, not to irritate it, because it's ok to irritate things, to keep them cool and wet, but we try not to irritate things, especially not wild animals that live in forests and parks, the places we're suppose to protect by putting those fires out, the way rangers do, always looking out for smoke and rushing to put it out, before it gets out of control, which you can do too, wherever you go, wherever you are, even asleep at night, when those alarms begin to sound, putting it out without a thought, and returning to a deep, restful sleep, secure in this awareness, that you can take care of you.

   (Terminate trance)

Migraine Headache Script

◆

Initiate this script after taking client into a least at medium state and continue to pace their breathing throughout the trance experience.

Now while you relax and allow yourself to experience the variety of changes that occur as you drift into a trance, I would like to help you to learn how to change those things that will allow you to be able to prevent or reduce your headaches, and the thing you need to learn is this, that when you feel a headache coming on, what you need to do is be able to allow your hands, and feet, to become very warm or hot very quickly, so as you pay attention to those hands and feet, I would like you to realize that you can imagine how it feels to have those hands and feet sitting in the hot rays of the sun…. or resting in the warm water of a bath…or whatever other image comes to mind when you begin to pay attention to that warmth there…and begin to feel the warmth grow, getting warmer and warmer, almost hot, comfortably swollen and warm, a warmth that may seem to spread into the arms and legs after a time, and as that warmth grows and becomes more clear in your awareness, you can continue to relax and drift down into a comfortable trance state, where your unconscious mind can find it's own way to let your mind become aware of that warmth and heaviness, a growing warmth and relaxation in the fingers of eyes are allowed to open.

(Terminate trance)

Tree Ants

◆

This script/metaphor could apply to those clients that need to increase their immune system responses to infections.

Take the client down in trance to a medium state and read the following script while pacing their breathing pattern.

There is a tree in Africa that has a special relationship with a particular kind of ant, the ants spend their entire lives living in that tree, they build their nests out of its leaves, they only drink the particular kind of sap that tree produces and secretes, or eats the tiny berries it grows. They never leave that tree, because that tree provides everything they need, and this type of ant is the only insect that does live in that tree, whenever any other insect begins to crawl upon it or lands on one of its leaves the ant sentries send out an alarm, and all the other ants come running, they attack those foreign bodies and either destroy them or drive them away, and in this way they protect their tree from any invaders that might attack it, or even destroy it, they save the tree, and the tree saves them, there are many other examples of the same thing throughout the world, where one tiny creature protects a large one from dangerous invaders, and in each and every case they always seem to have a way of paying very close attention to anything that could be harmful, so that they know immediately if some thing was wrong, and what is wrong and they pay close attention to it so they can do some thing about it, to eliminate or fix it, just the way people do when they notice a pain in a foot, and they pay close attention to that discomfort so they can tell what it is, and get rid of that stone in the shoe, as long as nothing gets in the way, and they continue to pay close attention to the way the body reacts and amplifies that reaction the way they amplify the sound of an engine, to hear what's wrong and let the body take care of itself with the same amazing grace that those ants take care of that tree, automatically and continuously, rushing to do those things needed to heal and protect.

(Continue intervention or terminate the trance)

Rafting

◆

This script/metaphor is good for use with clients who are bothered by hypertension.

Take the client down in trance to a medium state and read this script while pacing their breathing pattern.

When you take a raft trip or drift down the river in a canoe you begin to notice things that otherwise would go overlooked, especially those things that change the flow of the river, speed it up or slow it down, because when a river is wide and deep the water flows gently along, you can lie back with your eyes closed, listening to that quiet sound, but when the walls of the canyon begin to close in, and get narrower and narrower, the water rushes through faster and creates dangerous rapids, that you have to navigate carefully, until you get back to that place, where the river bed gets wide again, and deep peaceful quiet returns again, because water is just like anything else, the more you compress it, the faster it goes, as it flows along, and the bigger the space it has to fill, the calmer and quieter it becomes, and every child knows this too, they know when something is to small that they need to make it bigger to hold everything they have, so they get a bigger glass, or they get a bigger bowl, or they get a bigger pair of gloves so their hands can feel relaxed and comfortable, larger than they felt before, and everywhere inside expands to hold it all, such a wonderful feeling of relaxation, like loosening a tight belt after a huge meal, and feeling that relief, the pleasure of letting go, of letting things expand, feeling the new space provided, a new freedom to relax, the kind of quiet calmness you hear when those noisy children leave the room and go outside, and the teacher relaxes, the pressure relieved, even those old riverboats, with their paddle wheels and steam engines, could relieve some pressure by blowing their whistles when things got to hot inside, and everyone could relax on deck, watching the riverbanks go by, and the slow flow of the water in the deep channels they followed, taking their time to get from here to there, with nothing to do in the meantime except relax from the inside out, and feel the calm stillness of a quiet pool moving gently in the moonlight, while the soft sounds of evening drift by in an effortless flow, a calm slowing down to a gentle softness as relaxation continues and becomes a part of you.

(Continue intervention or terminate the trance)

Multiple Personalities Combined

◆

This is a good, short and direct approach for clients with a Multiple Personality Disorder.

Whichever personality is present, take down into trance to a medium state and read the following script. For maximum effect it is recommended you repeat this script in at least three separate hypnotic sessions.

As I speak to each of you together, there comes a time when it is time to decide now how to bring these things together, to join them together as one, to create a new life, a new beginning, not a starting over, but a change of pace, using what is useful now and letting go of the rest of it, so I would like to say to one of each of you, or each one of you, that I believe you have the ability to do what I suggest, to use this opportunity to evaluate what's there and to use what is useful from each other, to create a new, more complete one, and to erase the rest, and to do so very carefully, with the complete understanding that each part can be examined, and some things can be eliminated, while others are blended together to form a more comfortable you, to form a more useful you, to form a happier you than you've ever been before, and these things can seem to happen automatically, almost overnight, but in reality it happened carefully, trying on one thing, then another, until it comes out just right, then going on with things better than before, because things change over time. It is time to change you too. To stay the same from day to day, to be the same, to be what you can be now that you can join, say thanks and good-bye to some. saying hello to some, letting go of others, and become you. the very center of you, in a most becoming way, a way that allows you to be the very best you that you can be, a very happy you, the changes take place very fast slowly, and very comfortable, becoming the very center of you.

(Terminate trance)

Merging Script

◆

This script/metaphor is for use with clients with multiple personality disorders.

Take the client's base line personality in to trance to a medium state, pace their breathing as you tell them the following story.

As you drift, the mind drifts, like water from one place to another, automatically, effortlessly flowing, going the easiest way down toward the sea, and when you fly above it, you see the paths it takes, the tiny creeks and streams, that wind their way down the hills, down to the valleys below where they flow into the river, and that river flows along, getting larger and larger, gaining more and more from each new stream that joins it, and those rivers flow together, a larger river forms, and it flows too, it flows gently but surely towards the sea, it winds its way around mountains, it surges through the plains, gathering more and more strength, from other streams and rivers along the way, and eventually it reaches the bay, where it spreads throughout the delta and joins the power of the ocean, and becomes a part of that sea of life, a part of everything, and while you continue to relax, I would like to talk to all of you, to all the you's there are, because a bunch of yous' together can be a marvelous forest, and one you alone is just a tree in the middle of no where, when things join together they gain strength and protection from each other, it is a sign of the times, headlines in the newspaper each day describe the way small companies are forming large healthy companies by joining together, a merger of resources, several small banks announced a merger the other day and it was difficult to work out who would be in charge, but eventually they worked it out so that everyone was happy, everyone was represented, and each group had its say so that in a short time, when they change all their signs, and they change all the labels, no one will ever know that things weren't always that way, it will just seem to be the way it is supposed to be to be together as one, to be one, like a special color that is several colors blended together to be a new color, a special color all its own in that painting a portrait perhaps of a family, a group of people living as one, where each has special abilities, and each has a special purpose to serve, but sometimes they begin to keep secrets from each other and the world, and when that happens they are brought together and told to tell each other those secrets they all need to know, because when mother has a secret, or father has a secret, or brother or sister have secrets, and they all have secrets from outsiders, the family begins to fall apart, and each member loses something, because they all need each other, and they all need to be loved by each other, but secrets keep them from each other, and they begin to be mean to each other, when they need to tell each other they are very, very sorry and they need to come together, to cry together, to love together, to share their lives and strengths so that when they have their portrait painted, they look like they belong together as one, and the artist can merge the colors as the relief and relaxation of them all, allow the minds to drift together, winding gently but surely toward the sea, where each can see and feel that secure feeling of belonging, here and now, safe and sound, because things change as relaxation occurs.

(Terminate trance)

Dreams

◆

A script/metaphor for adult survivors of child sexual assault.

Take the client down in trance to at least a medium state and read the following script as you continue to pace the client's breathing pattern.

Now you have told me many things about your life, and listening to the truth about someone's life is a privilege and an honor, and though you don't need my thanks, I really do thank your conscious mind for sorting and categorizing so much information, and I thank your unconscious mind for what you can let your conscious mind discover later on, and there are so many things a person can discover, I remember the time five or six years ago when I first discovered what it would be like to live an entire life feeling different every day, because that's when I met Annie, and she was the only dwarf I had ever met, and I learned that in childhood it really hadn't been a problem because everyone was small and little then, but friends grew up and Annie stayed small, and had to go living her life in a world of big people, she had a special stool in the kitchen, she pushed it around as she moved from counter to cabinet, so she could jump on top of it and reach out for the things she needed, so she could look into the freezer, and reach the burners on the stove, she had a special sewing machine and she made all of her own clothes from her own designs since nothing else would fit, I really wanted to learn from her about living such a life, and she told me, there's just one thing you can say about people like me, there's always going to be something that comes up, and I thought a long time about that and what it might mean in a life, now a client I worked with a while back told me about a dream he had where he'd awaken in his bedroom, but the entire room was covered with a dense fog, and when he first felt the fog he was quite angry, finding himself damp and uncomfortable and unable to see a foot ahead of him, and the anger just grew and grew until he felt nothing but rage, and that heavy fog enveloping him, he wanted to run screaming from the room, but when he opened his mouth to speak nothing came out, and who would he tell? He was so alone, and how could there be so much fog? Would anyone believe him? These thoughts occupied his mind, he couldn't move, he couldn't cry, he could only feel his anger, rusting like a nail in the dense fog, and just when things seemed darkest he became aware of a breath of warm air hovering around his face, and you can imagine his surprise to discover that warm air, moist air was his own breath mingling with the fog, and he continued to breathe deep strong breaths, blowing that fog away with every inhalation as the fog lifted, and light began filtering into the room, anger lifting, breathing calmly, peacefully and he awaken from that dream with a new understanding, and it was about the same time that he realized that he was always in control of his situation.

(Terminate trance)

Meeting the Inner Child

◆

The purpose of this exercise is to assist the client in getting in touch with their inner child. This in itself should generate insight for the client as to what their present needs might be, and lend additional insight into lifelong behaviors.

Take client down in trance to a medium state and tell the client the following story pacing their breathing throughout trance.

Think back now to when you were 7 or 8 years old (Pause). Now picture in your mind the place you lived when you were that age (Pause). Now imagine that you are standing outside that very place looking at it, now walk around to the door you mainly used when you were a child, slowly now open the door and walk in, notice the sights, sounds and smells that were familiar to you (Pause), continue to walk to the room where you used to feel the most secure and comfortable in, there as that 7 or 8 year old child, notice what you are doing, how were you dressed? (Pause) Now tell the child the most important/valuable information that he or she can use in their coming years now that you are an adult and have lived those years (Pause). Go ahead now and speak to the child and tell them what they need to know (Pause). Now give the child a hug before you leave, if you can't hug the child, then just say good-bye. (Pause) Now turn and walk back out the same way you came in. Continue to walk to the location where you first viewed the place where you lived.

(Terminate trance, ensuring that you empower the client's memory)

You can expect this experience to be very impactful and profound for some clients. You need to ask your clients to explain their experience in detail to you from start to finish. This experience should help build insight and possibly identify issues to be resolved in the future.

Adults with Abusive Childhood Issues

◆

For those clients still bother by childhood abuse issues, physical, emotional and sexual.

Move the client down in trance to a medium state, read the following script slowly as you continue to pace the client's breathing throughout trance.

You know, and I know, that nothing can undo what happened to you in the past, what was to you was done to you back then, but that was then, and this is now, you can stop the pain and fear, you can put an end to it, now, and you already know how, you know to forget to pay attention to particular things, you know how to shut doors and windows on the past, you know how to see things now for what they are now, not what was, and your unconscious knows how to walk forward in time across that line, a boundary line that marks a new beginning, that lets you join the present, as you let go of the past, that lets you see a future, when you will remember how good it felt today to let go of that past, to say goodbye to it, and to let yourself feel ok. So go ahead now and keep going ahead later on, because that past is through and you are just you here and now, and when you get home, there is something you can do to put this away and get on with the future, some way for you, a ritual perhaps, a ceremonial letting go, throwing something away to let yourself know that the past is done and the future has begun, and you will do that, will you not?

(Terminate trance)

Saying Goodbye

◆

This is a script/metaphor for use with adult survivors of abusive childhoods, trauma.

Take the client down to a medium state of trance and read them the script while pacing their breathing.

As you continue to relax and experience the awareness of many different things, you may begin to wonder how many different ways there are to heal a wound, a wound from long ago that never healed, but remained behind to change the way you think and feel, like a woman I know who always wondered why she was the way she was, until one day she discovered a child within, a sad child, an unhappy child, an angry hurt child from long ago, a child she always heard in the background, a child she protected and did everything for today, a child who made her feel so sad, and she would do anything to keep that child quiet, to keep that child happy, to give that child what it wanted and needed, and I asked what needed to be done, and she said she needed to say good-bye to that child, she needed to hug that child, to hold that child, and to tell that child how very, very sorry she was that those things had happened to it, she felt so badly for the pain, so badly for the fear, so badly for the anger, but she knew she had to say good-bye, finally, she had to leave it behind and go on with her life, she knew there was nothing she could do to save that child, to change the past, to undo what was, and there was nothing she could do, so she hugged the child, and said good-bye and walked away, and cried and cried. The hardest thing she had ever done was to say good-bye, leave it behind, abandon it to the past, she felt awful, but she knew that was what she had to do, all she could do was watch the child slowly disappear, there was nothing she could do to change the past, it was beyond her control now, as it was in the past, nothing she could do to undo what that child went through, but afterwards she was free, felt free, to do what she wanted, the child was gone and she was free, free of the past, free to be, and so as you relax, and continue to drift down, your unconscious knows what you can do, or not do, your conscious knows too, and you can feel the freedom of that relaxed letting go in your own way, even as you drift more deeply at times than others.

(Terminate trance)

Letting Go

♦

This script/metaphor is good for clients who won't let go of abusive relationships, or repeating the same behavioral mistakes over and over.

Take the client into at least a medium state of trance, tell them this story while continuing to pace their breathing.

There was once a young Indian brave who climbed to the top of a snow covered mountain, upon reaching the top he came across a magical snake lying in the snow, the snake spoke to the young warrior, saying, would you please carry me down from this mountain top before I die of the cold, the young warrior was fearful at first, he told the snake that he was afraid that the snake would bite him, and the snake replied with a promise that he would not bite the warrior if he would carry him down from the mountain to safety, the young warrior wrapped the snake in a warm blanket and carried him down to the bottom of the mountain, when they reached the bottom of the mountain the warrior unwrapped the snake and set him free, and almost immediately the snake bit the young warrior, the warrior cried out, you promised not to bite me if I helped you, why did you bite me, the snake replied, you knew what I was before you picked me up.

The Rose

◆

This script/metaphor can be used with clients who have difficulty committing to relationships.

Take the client down in trance to a medium state and read this script while pacing their breathing pattern.

As you continue to relax, enjoying the beautiful feelings of trance, as it continues to spread over your entire body, feeling so wonderful, in your mind's eye I would like you to create a rose, a beautiful rose, notice the color, how very pretty, you can shape the rose to any form you desire, perhaps a bud, perhaps open and inviting, imagining the beautiful scent of that rose, how very nice, as you continue to enjoy the beautiful rose I would like to share something with you that I heard a long time ago, it was actually in the form of a song, but I do remember the words, the words held such great wisdom for me I felt they should be shared with you, the words were, Some say love is a river that drowns the tender reed, some say love, it is a razor that cuts deep and leaves your heart to bleed, some say love, it is a hunger an endless searching need, I would say, it is a flower, and you its only seed, its the heart afraid of breaking, that never learns to dance, its the dream afraid of waking, that never takes the chance, its the one who won't be taken, who can not seem to give, the soul afraid of dying that never learns to live, when the night has been to lonely, and the road has been to long, and you think that love is only for the lucky and the strong, just remember in the winter far beneath the bitter snow lies the seed that with the sun's love in the spring becomes a rose, a rose, beautiful, very pretty and desirable, but so very fragile in appearance, and in reality a very durable and strong flower, we all possess the seed deep in side ourselves to grow into a beautiful and strong rose, year after year the rose returns, just as we choose to do, another old saying comes to mind, nothing ventured, nothing gained, just as the rose ventures forth to be loved and admired, we find our happiness's through venturing out, perhaps a small venture at first, then possibly a bigger venture latter, not too late though as we don't want to wait to long to venture forth in search of our happiness, even the misfortunes of the past can not hold us back from searching for that elusive thing called happiness, nothing ventured, nothing gained.

(Continue with the intervention or terminate trance)

The Dance

◆

This script/metaphor could be helpful for your clients who have a problem/fear with risk taking.

Take the client into a medium state of trance and slowly read the script while pacing the breathing pattern.

Judy and Jane were both high school girls who were getting set to go to the high school dance on an upcoming Friday night, Judy was wondering what it was going to be like at the dance, this would be the first one she had attended, Jane, on the other hand, was very confident, she knew about these things, she had heard about dances from her older brothers and sisters, she knew what to expect and how to dress, what to do, Judy had to wonder and be curious about what she would find out at the dance that night, the more she thought, the more she wondered if she could go there and have the evening be a success, she really wouldn't know until she found the secret of the four letter words that ended in "k", as the days got closer, Jane had already picked out her dress and what she would be wearing to the dance, Judy didn't know, she was concerned about colors, size and style, Jane just got more and more excited about who she'd be seeing at the dance, what they'd be wearing, and who'd be with whom, Judy however, became more and more anxious not knowing whether she would look all right, whether she would make an awkward mistake, maybe even step on someone's toes, she would soon find out that all would be okay, after she learned the secret of the four letter words ending in "k", Jane was talking at school to all her friends, getting all the information of who was going to be with who, what everybody was wearing, how people were going to get there, whom they were traveling with, Judy didn't want to talk about the dance, as it got closer and closer, she got more and more anxious, she didn't know what would transpire that night, whether somehow she'd be made to look foolish, or maybe not look right, but she would soon find out when she had the secret of the four letter words, the night of the dance, Judy and Jane came in the same car, Jane was very confident that she was wearing the right dress and appropriate accessories, Judy was still not knowing what would happen when she found the secret of the four letter words, during the course of the evening, both girls danced a little, as they danced, Judy felt better and better, not knowing that the secret of the four letter words that ended in "k" would shortly be revealed to her, she was curious about how the dance would turn out, whether she would leave the dance with somebody, or go back home with Jane's mother, at one point, the dejay announced that the next dance would be "ladies choice", Jane of course, had no difficulty going right over and picking out the captain of the football team, Judy hesitated at first, and as she did, she opened her purse to take out a Kleenex and wipe her brow, inside she saw that her mother had left two words on the Kleenex, those two words were "risk" and "pick", she walked up to a quarterback she was interested in getting to know and asked him to dance, she smiled at him, he smiled back, as they walked onto the dance floor together, Judy felt very proud of herself, almost a sense of relief that those two magic words, risk and pick had been revealed at exactly the right time, she may have made some mistakes, but that's part of risking, if you risk, you don't know what you might get, but you know that when you don't risk, you won't get anything, Judy and Bob continued to dance together all evening, dance after dance, she had found a new friend and all because of the two secret four letter words that ended in "k", and though Jane had a nice time too, just as she had expected to, when she left the dance that night, it wasn't with an additional feeling of exuberance and pride that accompanies an opportunity to achieve something you hadn't expected, but can really appreciate, and Judy was as happy about that as she was about the date she and Bob had arranged for the next evening.

(Continue intervention or terminate trance)

Emotional Droughts

◆

A script/metaphor for a client who has difficulties with making emotional commitments.

Take the client down in trance to a medium state and read the script while pacing their breathing.

There are some plants that find it easier to survive a drought because they have deep roots burrowed down into the soil, down where it stays damp and moist even when the ground is hard and dry, but most grasses have shallow roots, fine roots that go down just below the surface, so they dry out when the rains stop and are unable to get nutrients, the things they need to stay alive, because once the nutrients stop flowing in, the growing stops as well and the drying starts, just like any living tissue which is why you loosen a tourniquet once every three or four minutes and let the blood flow through again to nourish the cells and to take away the waste, even though the bleeding starts again, because we all have lots of blood and we can stand to lose a bit, but we can't stand to block the flow of those things needed for very long, and the marvel of it all is that we can donate to each other, we can give each other what we need and never miss it at all, the way a plant with deep roots can give us moisture even in a drought, while shallow rooted grass becomes dry and rough and tends to catch fire, like the grasslands of California where fire is always a hazard, but it is a different state of mind to be in a place where you can play and enjoy the sea breezes in the fertile valleys that are so close to the ocean, but still need to be irrigated so that the ground can support the gardens that feed an entire nation and provide the fruits we enjoy in the winter months, so much food they could never eat it all, so they don't need to hoard it, they can share it, sell it, and reap great profits in return, because no one would say they should just give it all away because they need to save some just for themselves, and they need to get something out of it just for themselves, but they seem to be very proud of all they provide for others, things from deep inside the center of that state and the more taxes that they pay the more they know they earned that day, but nobody likes withholding money just to throw it away with no return on their investment, so sometimes they put it away, deep in vaults in the biggest banks, to keep it safe for later.

Playgrounds in the Mind

◆

This script/metaphor is for couples with issues of insecurity and trust in their relationship.

Take the clients down in trance to a medium state and read the following script while pacing the breathing.

Each of you has a brain that you use in every day life, that thinks, and understands and remembers, and you depend on it, to provide you with the abilities needed, to take care of things for you, but I wonder if you know that the neurons in that brain can inhibit each other or excite each other so that when some neurons fire they excite others, but when other neurons fire they inhibit the others and keep them from responding at all, and so there are times when the harder those cells try to do one thing, the more difficult it becomes, while at other times not doing anything at all gives the desired results, and if one neuron is stimulated to much, it may become exhausted and stop responding completely, just like the cells in a muscle that gets tired of doing the same thing over and over again, this is even true for little children, who may be afraid at first when their parents take them to the playground and turn them loose to run around, you can watch that tiny toddler, unsure of its self at first, unsure of the parent too, afraid that the parent may disappear if it gets to far away, so at first you go with them, you reassure them that it is ok to go off to play in the sandbox or to explore the swings, and that toddler keeps coming back, but staying away longer and longer, beginning to play with others, even getting on the teeter totter and learning how to balance, each trusting the other not to get off suddenly, the kind of trust it takes to invest your life's savings in a business with a friend, not the kind of thing you would do with a total stranger, but there are some people who we know we can trust because they have earned that trust like interest in a bank that you count on to be there, even though you know that banks do fail sometimes, but it is pretty rare, so we trust them, unless we have good reason not to, just like the child trusts others, they are all friends unless they prove they are not, and when that friend gets tired of doing the same thing over and over, they go off together and do something else, on the swings or in the sandbox, knowing their parents are there, waiting at the picnic bench to take them home when they're tired, to bring them back when they're not, and because that all goes without saying, they can enjoy themselves quite completely.

(Continue with intervention or terminate trance)

Jealous Ways

◆

This script/metaphor is a short and direct approach for helping clients deal with their feelings of jealousy.

Take the client down in trance to a medium state and read the script while pacing their breathing pattern.

Now you say that you recognize that you're to jealous, and I know what you need to do, if you really want to avoid that problem, but you won't want to do it, unless you really believe that (he) (she) merits your trust, and so the first thing to do is this: Decide now, here and now, once and for all, does this person deserve you, and deserve your love, or not? If they do, then they are trustworthy, if they don't, then you'd better get out, right now, as soon as you can, but if they are trustworthy enough to deserve you and your devotion, then here is what you need to do, because your jealousy is the meanest, the most obnoxious thing you can do to someone who cares about you, you need to apologize to that person, in every way you can, you need to get down on your knees, and tell them how sorry you are, for being so mean and cruel, for even thinking they could betray you, for not accepting their gift to you, because if you don't love them, then let go of them, and if you do love them, then you'd better say your sorry, and be adult enough to let them be an adult too, because if you keep acting like a mean, suspicious parent, its quite apparent to me, that you're using your imagination in a very unpleasant way, in ways that are quite painful to those you say you love, so the first step is to apologize for being so mean and cruel, for using your imagination in such a childish way, without any control at all, and you certainly should apologize for soiling this sacred ground, and creating a foul odor in the atmosphere of love, because you will feel so embarrassed if you do it again, that your face will flush, and you will blush, and that will be the last time you try to control what doesn't belong to you, but is a gift, a loan, that will be repossessed if you don't treat it right, so decide now what you're going to do, and what you're not going to do, and see if you have enough to do it, no matter what.

(Terminate trance)

Territory

◆

This script/metaphor is for clients/couples who have a problem dealing with jealousy.

Take the clients down into trance to a medium state and begin reading this script while pacing their breathing pattern. Pace the client with the slowest breathing pattern.

As each of both of you continue to listen to me, I can begin to wonder if either or both of you, separately or together, have ever had the experience of watching a dog mark out its territory, because dogs, and many other animals, spend a lot of time establishing boundaries, using scents to say this belongs to me, some animals have special glands that give off a peculiar scent, and others just urinate here and there, and then act like that land belongs to them, the same way countries put up fences, and draw imaginary lines on maps, and then say that everything here belongs to us, for us to use any way we want, and everyone here has to do what we want, whether they want to or not, they have to do what the dictator says, until there is a revolution or the people move some place else, or the dictator changes the rules and lets the people do as they want, lets the people make the decisions and declare freedom throughout the land, which requires a lot of faith and trust that the people will do what's best, and won't just up and leave as soon as they have the chance, but if that leader believes in them and they believe in their leader, if they respect each other and themselves, then democracy seems to work and people vote for who they like best, like a popularity contest or the way we select our favorite movie stars, who seem to be one thing, but turn out to be another, one of the things you learn as a therapist is that things sometimes are not what they seem, we imagine how happy the rich folks are, and we think we know what goes on there, but when you really talk to people, in private where they tell the truth, you discover what we imagine is rarely accurate or even close, and that we can imagine anything, but that doesn't make it so, even though we can find evidence for it, in trashy papers and magazines, what we really see behind the scenes is that everyone needs something special, and that all the boundaries dissolve, when the dog finally lets you pet him, and you play with him for awhile, he doesn't growl any more when you cross his urinary line, or enter into his territory with a bone or something sweet, and you let him lick your hand, so that later on that friendship allows each of you to come and go as you wish, comfortable in the knowledge that there is a trust in each other you can bank on, and that it makes good sense an is in your best interest to do so.

(Continue with intervention or terminate trance)

Treasures of the Past

◆

This script/metaphor is good for clients who have lost a significant someone or some part of themselves.

Take the client to at least a medium state of trance and read the script while pacing their breathing pattern.

I wonder if you have ever seen the small fragile glass figurines that artisans sell at fairs and in shopping malls, made of tiny strands of clear bright glass all carefully laced together to form the shape of a ship or an animal, or even a house or a tree, that seemed to fascinate children with their delicate sparkles and shapes, like priceless jewels, valuable possessions, to be carried in velvet cases and protected, kept safe from loss or damage, tiny treasures, a gift to someone, like the treasure carried in ships across the sea, there was a program on TV several years ago, about a man who spent twenty years searching for such a ship, a lost treasure ship, one of hundreds that had been lost along the coast because of accidents and disasters and wars, he researched it very carefully, and though he knew exactly what had been lost, he also thought he knew what happened and where the treasure had sunk, but it was hard to find that ship, it had been lost for so long, it had gotten buried with mud and coral, and there were many other wrecks in the area, any one of which could have been the one, but wasn't, so he spent many years searching, and he raised thousands of dollars from investors, because he was convinced that there was something of great value down there. a lost treasure of immeasurable worth, and he convinced others it was there too, one day the divers returned to the surface shouting and screaming and holding up gold bars, they had found that ship, and it contained more than you could imagine, tons of gold bars, silver bars, gold coins, treasures untold, things from the past that had gone untouched, that had not been seen for hundreds of years suddenly were there for people to hold and to feel, and they held them with reverence, touching them gently and silently, as if these things that had been lost for so long, contained some memory of the past, something special that people need, something special to protect, like those tiny glass figures that you see at fairs and malls, they seem to be so fragile, so easily broken by someone rough, but they actually are quite sturdy and can survive for years and years, even when lost or hidden away, like the treasures at the bottom of the ocean, hidden deep down below, something precious and valuable inside, a part of you before, that belonged to you before, and the joy of its discovery, the recovery of that buried treasure, the pleasure of knowing it belongs to you, something you can bring back with you, that warm good part of the heart of the matter that children sometimes lose for a time, or have taken from them at another time, but it always lies there waiting to be brought back to the surface where it can be touched and protected and kept close to you forever, because it all belongs to you.

The Turtle

♦

This script/metaphor is helpful for those who feel they have to control the other person in their relationship, and have decided they want to give up their control.

Take the client down in trance to a medium state and read the script while pacing their breathing pattern.

As you continue to relax, enjoying the beautiful feelings of trance, there is a story I know that I wanted to share with you, I'm sure in the story you will find much wisdom, the story is about a little boy and his turtle, the boy and his turtle were very close to each other and spent much of the summer days together, on the first day of school the little boy told his turtle that it had to stay in the house until he returned from school in the evening, and that evening when the little boy returned from school he discovered the turtle outside the house, the little boy scolded the turtle for disobeying, and told the turtle if he left the house without him that he would surely lose his friend, someone else would take the turtle for their friend, and then he would be alone, so the next day when the boy returned from school the turtle was outside the house again, once again the boy scolded the turtle, the next morning before the boy left for school he put the turtle in a tire in the back yard with food and water to protect the turtle, again, when he returned from school that evening he found that the turtle had gotten out of the tire and was in the front yard waiting for him, the little boy was getting upset because he couldn't seem to control the turtle, so he built a wooden box with tall sides to contain his turtle while he was away from home, the next morning the boy put the turtle in the wooden box and commanded him to remain there until he returned from school that evening, upon the boy's return to home that evening, he once again found that the turtle had gotten free and was in the front yard waiting for him, the little boy was so upset, he was certain if he didn't control the turtle he would lose his best friend, the next morning before leaving for school the little boy felt desperate and nearly out of ideas to control his friend the turtle, before leaving for school the boy drove a nail into the turtle's hard shell, and attached a long string to it that he tied to a tree in the backyard, he felt confident now that the turtle would not wander about while he was gone, that evening when the little boy returned from school, he found his poor turtle in the front yard, bleeding and dying from pulling loose from the nail, just laying there about to die, waiting for his friend to return.

(Terminate trance)

The Flat Tire

---◆---

This script/metaphor is good for clients who have trouble accepting people without negative stereotyping.

Take the client down in trance to a medium state and read this script as you pace their breathing pattern.

As you continue to enjoy all the beautiful feelings of trance there is a short story I want to share with you, a story that teaches wisdom, your unconscious mind will recognize the wisdom and put it to work for you, there is a story I use to tell whenever I would be teaching a group of young counselors about one day when I was driving across town to attend a meeting, as I was going down the street I suddenly noticed I had a flat tire, I pulled over to the side of the road, and got out of my car and walked around it, no one needs a flat tire on a busy day, as I got the spare tire and tools out of the trunk, to my surprise, I noticed that I was parked right in front of the state mental hospital, and one of the mental patients was leaning out of the window watching me, I just thought to myself, another crazy, stupid person, I went on about the business of getting my tire changed, taking the flat off, and then putting the spare back on, when I went to put the lug nuts on the tire I discovered that the lug nuts had rolled down into the storm drain, I was so upset, I cursed the car, and even kicked it a few times, the mental patient who had been leaning out the window watching me all this time yelled and got my attention, he said mister, why don't you just take one lug nut from each of the other tires and put them on until you get to the next gas station, I thought to myself, why didn't I think of that? I told the fellow that it was a great idea, but I couldn't understand why he was a patient in a mental hospital if he could figure out the solution to my problem, the mental patient replied, I may be crazy, but I'm not stupid, it seemed that most every student in my class could draw some wisdom from my experience, everyone is not as they seem, while some may, some may not, you have the wisdom to know.

(Terminate trance)

About the Author

Randy Hartman currently holds a masters degree in human relations from the University of Oklahoma. Randy has spent more than twenty five years as a hypnotherapist, addictions counselor and in mental health counseling. To date he has written five books on the subject of hypnosis.